CHALLENGER'S
WAR

CLIVE HOPKINS

First published in Great Britain in 2008
Pen Press
25 Eastern Place
Brighton, BN2 1GJ

ISBN13: 978-1-906710- 04-0

Printed and bound in the UK by Cpod, Trowbridge, Wiltshire
A catalogue record of this book is available from
the British Library

Challenger's War is a work of fiction.
With the obvious exceptions of General Douglas MacArthur,
Admiral Joy, his named staff officers, Prime Ministers Churchill
and Attlee and US President Harry Truman, all characters in this
publication are fictitious and any resemblance to real persons,
living or dead, is purely coincidental.

Cover design by Jacqueline Abromeit

ABOUT THE AUTHOR

Clive Hopkins joined HMS Ganges at the age of fifteen and served in the Royal Navy in Destroyers, Frigates and Minesweepers in the Baltic, the Mediterranean and the Far East. He took part in actions off Malaya and Korea and was an observer at the British nuclear tests on the Monte Bello Islands off Australia's northern coast.

After leaving the RN, Clive married and lived in Canada for some time before returning to the UK and making a career in technical journalism.

He is currently working with the Historic Warships Volunteer Group, preserving and restoring HMS Cavalier, the last of the RN's WWII Emergency Class Destroyers afloat. HMS Cavalier (now in The Chatham Historic Dockyard) still wears the Royal Navy's White Ensign and is a Memorial to the 143 RN Destroyers lost to enemy action in World War Two and to the young men who went down in them.

AUTHOR'S NOTE

On November 14th, 2007, HRH Prince Philip, the Duke of Edinburgh KG, KT - known to many of his fellow ex-servicemen as the Iron Duke - attended the unveiling and dedication of the long-delayed, National Destroyer Memorial in Chatham's Historic Dockyard.

This impressive bronze lists and illustrates the 143 Royal Navy destroyers sunk during WWII and the men who died in them; many of them based at Chatham. Separated by a few feet and an integral part of this memorial, stands the last of these workhorses of the fleet, HMS Cavalier. Still afloat and now once again proudly wearing the white ensign of the Royal Navy. It is sixty five years since her keel was laid down at Samuel White's shipyard on a war-torn Isle of Wight.

Cavalier took part in the infamous Russia Convoys and subsequently served in the Far East against the Japanese but the march of time and technological progress could not be halted and in 1973 she was retired from active service.

Rescued, later, from a proposed sale to a Malaysian theme park operator, Cavalier was purchased and returned to her home-port of Chatham* to be lovingly restored and refurbished by small group of now elderly volunteers, many though not all of them ex-destroyer men.

These volunteers enjoyed meeting the Prince and met each other again some days afterwards for their annual end of year lunch. Loyal toasts were drunk, several tots consumed and stories told of 'the old days' when those present were young and in many cases served in Cavalier or ships like her. A few had actually served during the second world war in sister ships to Cavalier and a special toast was drunk to them in the belief that, had they not won that now long ago war on our behalf, we would not have been sitting there eating and drinking in good company.

Challenger's War is a fictionalised retelling of some of the many stories told of the destroyer service when, so shortly after their victory over Japan, ships like Cavalier were hurriedly withdrawn from the Reserve Fleet, experienced men were recalled from civvy street and together again with their regular service colleagues, were called upon to fight under the pale blue flag of the United Nations, in Korea. The tradition of the service was never better served.

* This is a story well worth the telling but better told by the Cavalier Association who achieved the impossible.

ACKNOWLEDGEMENTS

My thanks to members of the Korean Veteran's Association and to the Chatham Dockyard Historic Warships Restoration Volunteers for their expert technical assistance, their encouragement and their approval. My thanks also to The Historic Dockyard Chatham for allowing me access to HMS Cavalier, the last of the RN's 'Challenger' type Destroyers still afloat. Without these aides memoire, writing this book would have been much more difficult.

Where are the young lions of yesteryear
where are the brave young men that we were
where are the friends, all long since gone
those who were heroes – every one.

They are our dreams, our memories
with whom we fought our enemies
those we remember not as old as we are
but as the young lions of yesteryear

ONE

Through his binoculars, Challenger's captain watched the American aircraft circling over a target that he couldn't see, some way inland from the coast. Probably, he thought, a supply convoy from the north, making its way down to the front, to the line beyond which General MacArthur had decreed that no North Korean should pass; whatever the cost.

He could see nothing more than a little smoke; they must have hit something but from that altitude, possibly nothing more than some poor peasant farmer's home. This was no way to fight a war, no way to ensure that the apolitical peasants loved democracy any more than they had their earlier subjection by the Japanese or their king before that. It probably mattered little to them who was in power in Seoul, their way of life had changed little in a thousand years and, if the United Nations meant to fight its way back up the peninsula to the 38th parallel, it would probably take that long to do it; in an old fashioned, slug it out campaign, the Russian supplied and Chinese supported North Koreans could win.

He didn't like being little more than an observer, there had to be a better way. "Not what you might call exciting, is it?"

The officer of the watch nodding in agreement said, "Not unless you're underneath that lot, looking up."

A thousand miles from her new base at Kure in southern Japan, Challenger is one of a Flotilla of British destroyers pressed into the service of the recently formed United Nations. Her orders are simple, to protect the reputedly non-communist inhabitants of the nearby, strategically valuable South Korean islands from invasion by the Peoples Army of North Korea, now being bombed by the Americans only a few miles away on the mainland.

Second in command of the Flotilla, under Captain Bob Larkin, 'Captain D8' in Cossack, Challenger's captain, Commander David Powers, had been lucky enough to survive World War Two and clever enough to have risen to his present position. Whilst he felt secure in his expectation of further progress, given the time and the luck; regrettably, he thought, this duty was probably that least likely to provide any opportunity for that lady to show herself. "Stand down Action Stations," he told the officer of the watch. "Revert to Defence Stations."

Always a destroyer man, Powers knew he was popular with his fellow officers and respected by the ship's company as a man with no 'side'; Challenger is regarded as a happy ship, a good ship to be in; even if she had been built for as little as possible and therefore lacked in any sign of comfort. She should have been scrapped years ago.

Challenger, like the other ships in the flotilla, took her turn to patrol the inshore shallows of the Yellow Sea between the islands of the Paengnyong-do group and Cho-do, and was taking every opportunity to relieve the boredom by bombarding anything that moved on the communist held mainland shore.

Occasional trains ran the gauntlet between the end of one tunnel and the beginning of the next on the coastal railway line and were looked forward to by the gunners as ducks in an oversized shooting gallery. Unofficially, bets were laid upon the number of hits each gun's crew could score before the speeding train disappeared but everyone knew that the main railways were on the other side of Korea, on the east coast; this was a sideshow.

The American Admiral, from Tokyo, ensured that his ships got the prime targets and the publicity that followed in the world's newspapers. Professional publicists aboard their major ships ensured that the folks back home in the good old US of A knew what a great job their sailors are doing.

Back home in England, public attention focussed not upon this unwanted and unpopular new war but upon the continuing, everyday shortages, restrictions and food rationing imposed eleven years before.

Many of these had been retained and some even extended by the post-war Labour Government elected in nineteen forty-five with a landslide majority but now, after five years, increasingly regarded as a disastrous mistake. Here, there were no shortages, food was plentiful and good and the women friendly. To many aboard Challenger, though not to Commander David Powers her captain, war here was better than being at home.

For a moment, just a moment, he thought of home. Home and Sable, the girl he had married only days before he had left her to take command of this ship. Would she still love him when he returned? It would be at least another two years; he would write another chapter in his continuing letter to her tonight. Like all sailors, he added to a continuing letter whenever he could; a letter that would only end and be posted when he returned to port.

In that other war, the war that had seemed to last for ever, the war that had finally been won only five short years ago, he had had another wife; Helen. He had loved her as only a young man can love a young woman, totally, completely and as he had thought then, everlastingly. At least, this time, Sable would be in no danger. Helen, his lovely Helen, had been in the Portsmouth hospital in nineteen forty, helping to clean up the casualties as they were brought in from what remained of their homes when the bomb had blown it and her to smithereens.

He could see it still although he had not been there at the time. He had been at sea, where else would a sailor be in wartime? He had been at sea in a ship equipped to conduct a war against the German u-boats hunting in packs to destroy the allied convoys but at least he had had a chance. The odds were uneven but at least he could sometimes hear the u-boat coming and attack it before it could attack his charges, the unarmed, over-laden merchant ships in his care. Helen, his lovely Helen had had no chance. The bomber, thousands of feet above her had not selected either the hospital or Helen as his target; he had simply released his bombs over Portsmouth, hoping to hit something vital in the dockyard. It wasn't really his fault that one of his bombs had overshot the target area and hit the hospital.

It had taken nearly ten years to heal the wound, years in which he had fought the enemy on two fronts; as a naval officer and as a personal crusade to destroy those that had destroyed his wife and as he had believed at the time, his reason for living. He had thought that he would never forget nor forgive but he had, he had had to; life would have been impossible if he had continued to nurture his hatred

Slowly, very slowly, the wound had healed. First just a scab formed over the open weeping gash in his heart then, as more and more of the enemy were killed by his and other ships, the hurt slowly faded into the background; became just a nagging ache when he relaxed, when he tried to sleep. The war ended, promotion came and with it greater responsibilities and then, at someone else's wedding, he had met Sable.

Damn silly name, he had thought but pretty. They had both been alone and had drifted together rather than stand about like spare numbers. She was younger but recognised in him a man that she could like, perhaps even grow to love. He had found the table with all the Champaign and had taken one over to where she had been standing, looking out of the window. Somehow it had just gone on from there; neither of them forcing the pace, allowing nature to take its course.

Now, it was all starting again, another war, local now but one that, if not stopped here and now, could evolve into another all encompassing world conflict; a conflict of ideologies; this time, territorial conquest was secondary.

"Bridge, Plot." A disembodied voice issued from the voicepipe beside the binnacle behind which the officer of the watch was standing. "Radar shows a small vessel approaching from the north. Speed about eight knots, range about ten miles."

The officer of the watch, Lieutenant Brothers, punched the red klaxon button sounding the action stations alarm. Throughout the ship, watertight doors were again slammed shut and clipped. Guns crews, additional lookouts and other specialists closed up at their action stations on the upper deck whilst below, stewards, cooks and storemen slide down the steel ladders into the magazines, to feed the shells and their cordite cartridges into the hoists which would take them up to the now fully re-manned guns. On the bridge, Brothers bent over to speak into the voicepipe.

"Thank you Plot, what do you think? Fast patrol boat hoping to sneak up on us at sampan speed or one of their armed junks going flat out"?

"No way of knowing yet Sir, too small a target."

"Keep an eye on it eh? I don't want any surprises."

He mentally ticked off the 'closed-up' reports as they came in from all over the ship before turning to the captain who, sitting quietly in his wooden highchair at the back of the open bridge could see all and hear all without getting into anybody's way.. "Ship closed up at action stations, Sir."

"Thank you. I'll take her now."

It was Challenger's turn to be nearest to the mainland and the communist's guns and Powers was in no hurry to find himself sandwiched between a gunboat or possibly a torpedo boat to seaward and any waiting shore-side batteries. At eight knots, it would be about half an hour before the radar contact on a converging course reached them; there would be time to check it out.

"Yeoman," he turned to the yeoman of signals who had closed up at his action stations position on the bridge, "signal to Chop Suey. Request helicopter search of – give them the boat's position – suspected Red warship."

The People's Army's naval base at Namp'o further to the north was limited in its capacity but armed junks and FPB's, Russian built fast patrol boats, made what often amounted to suicidal attacks against the allied occupied islands and even the faster and better armed allied warships. Usually they relied on fog or darkness to shroud their approach so perhaps it was foggy to the north. In that case, the American army chopper from the carefully hidden 'Chop Suey' base on one of the outer islands would see nothing but it was worth a try; cooperation between the navy and the US army was to be encouraged anyway, you never knew when it might just be necessary. The navigating officer gave the yeoman the approaching boat's position.

Continuing her patrol, Challenger's lookouts searched the shoreline for any signs of troops or gun emplacements, any kind of target that could justify shooting off a few more shells. The sooner they ran short of ammunition, the sooner they could go back to Kure or perhaps the other, nearer new base at Sasebo to rearm and get a few cold beers inside them.

In the three weeks they had been on patrol, they had expended more than two hundred 4.5in shells and a great deal more 40mm Bofors ammunition. No slouch when it came to engaging the enemy, if there was any chance, any chance at all, of inflicting damage on the enemy then Commander David

Powers R.N could be relied upon. He, like his ship's company was bored with the constant patrolling up and down and any break in the monotony was welcome; even this appearance of a small, presumably enemy, vessel on the radar. You never knew, something might come of it.

"When's Anzac due to relieve us Yeo?"

From his position on the starboard side of the ship's open bridge, Leading Signalman Hawkins was watching the bearing on which the radar detected contact would appear any minute now and was largely making conversation. It didn't matter to him when the Aussies relieved them except that they would then move out to seaward, a little further from the shore-side guns; some of these, the 76mm buggers, could do a lot of damage if they got the range right. There was only so much good luck in the world and they hadn't been hit yet; it must be Challenger's turn soon.

"Tomorrow Harry but don't you worry about them, you just keep your eyes peeled for this damned boat that the radar can see and we can't."

"Why can't the Yankee whirlybird see them, for God's sake? They were told where to look."

"Ah yes but, I expect they had to finish their Coca Cola and ice cream before they could go and take a look. I'm sure they'll tell us where it is just after we've sunk it."

"Hope so, Yeo. Still, the signal said we were to cooperate with the Yanks whenever possible so that they know we're here. Otherwise they might go and make another Hollywood film about how they won this war single handed, just like the last one."

A whistle sounded up the voice pipe beside him. The telegraphist's voice from the wireless office below called. "Signal in the bucket."

The voice pipe was their main means of communication with the wireless office two decks down and a little rubber bucket on a length of string allowed them to pass messages up and down more quickly than any messenger could run.

Yeoman Houser hauled the bucket up and flattened out the message sheet. He placed it on his clipboard and offered it to the captain, reading it as he did so.

"Junk, Sir. No sign of armament."

"Thank you Yeoman." He picked up the microphone for the ship's Tannoy PA system. "Junk bearing red three seven, range four miles. All guns train on that bearing."

"Guns", he turned to the gunnery officer, "are you all tooled up as they say in the movies?"

"All ready Sir. Main armament is loaded with HE rather than armour piercing, didn't think we would need that; torpedo tubes loaded too Sir, just in case."

"Hope you're right Guns. You don't think that perhaps 'B' gun might try semi-armour piercing? Just to put my mind at rest."

The gunnery officer spoke into his microphone. "'B' gun reload with SAP, repeat 'B' gun only reload SAP."

The captain of 'B' gun repeated the order back to him then confirmed that 'B' gun had reloaded.

"Got him Sir, right on the bearing. Definitely a junk and there's no visible activity on deck. Looks like a civvy boat Sir. Can't see any guns anywhere."

"Thank you Hawkins. How many civilian junks have we seen around here?"

"Ah, well, none Sir, I see what you mean."

"Then, for the purposes of this exercise, I think we can safely assume that she's hostile."

The port lookout, using more powerful binoculars than Hawkins reported. "I think I saw someone for'ard, Sir. Don't know what he was doing but he disappeared under what looks like a tarpaulin just for'ard of the foremast."

"Thank you."

"Guns, try a shot across her bows."

"'A 'gun, one round, ranging shot ahead of target. Shoot."

The ding-ding of the gun-firing bell sounded a split second before the bang. They all watched the fall of shot almost on top of but just in front of the target.

"Good shot Guns."

The junk turned towards, shortening her silhouette and presenting a smaller target. "Ah, now I regard that as a hostile act Guns. If she was a civvy as the Leading Signalman here suggested, I would have expected her to drop her sails a bit sharpish and wave something white at us; wouldn't you?"

"Yes Sir, I think I would."

"They're removing the tarpaulin Sir. Can't see what's under it though."

"Thank you lookout. Shit! I can. They've got some sort of torpedo tube thingy rigged up under there and I think they mean to shoot at us. Guns. Any time you're ready you may shoot at her."

"Why thank you Sir, that's most kind. Main armament; five rounds, shoot, shoot, shoot."

The ding-ding of firing bells came almost simultaneously from all four 4.5 in. guns and the junk disintegrated in a shower of wood and cordage.

The Gunnery Officer pressed the tit on his microphone again "Check, check, check."

In the silence that followed, the lookout's call sounded louder than it really was. "Torpedo! Bearing red two five Sir."

"Thank you lookout. Wheelhouse," the captain spoke down the second voice pipe beside the binnacle, "port twenty"

"Port twenty Sir."

"Steer 315."

The coxswain in the wheelhouse below repeated back the order and spun the wheel, catching it and steadying on the course ordered. "Course 315 Sir."

Everyone on the bridge watched as the single torpedo sliced down the starboard side, only a matter of feet away from the ship.

"Bit close, I think, Guns. Next time, do try to sink him before he fires at us, will you?"

"Yeoman Signal to Chop Suey. Your unarmed junk just fired a torpedo at me but thanks anyway." He lent over the voice pipe again. "Wheelhouse, Coxswain, steer 325. You may stand down. Pipe hands revert to Defence Stations."

"Course 325, hands revert to Defence Stations, very good Sir." The ship swung to starboard, resuming her previous course.

"Course 325 Sir."

The captain on the bridge heard the click of the Tannoy system being switched on in the wheelhouse and the bosun's call trilling before the broadcast. "Hands to defence stations."

"Yeoman, signal to C in C, attacked by torpedo equipped junk in position – get that from the navigating officer – junk destroyed by gunfire. No need for any priority Yeoman, send it 'Routine'." He smiled at Lieutenant 'DD' Darling the navigating officer, "I wonder what they'll think of next, pilot."

He turned to the officer of the watch, "OK Brother, she's all yours, I'll be in my cabin if you need me."

*   *   *

With first light, their relief came into sight, she had been seen on the ship's radar some time before and her arrival was awaited with pleasure.

From the bridge of the approaching destroyer, HMAS Anzac, a signal light flashed. Yeoman Houser, up for his early morning check that all was well with his department, stepped up to the ten inch signal light on Challenger's port side and flashed him a 'K', to carry on.

"Anzac has mail for us, Sir," he reported.

"Thank you Yeoman. That will make a few of the hands happy, I imagine." The officer of the watch bent over the voice pipe that led directly to the Captain's sea cabin. "Anzac in sight Sir, says she has mail for us. "

"OK. I'll be right up. Ask them to come alongside port side to."

"Port side to, Sir. Very good."

"Yeoman. Ask Anzac to come alongside port side to, please."

The light flashed again and the Australian ship acknowledged.

"Morning. This'll please some of the troops, eh?"

The Captain acknowledged the salute from the officer of the watch and sat in his wooden highchair behind the binnacle. It would be the only salute he would receive that day from Lieutenant 'Taffy' Evans; the custom on ships being to salute the Captain just once per day, at first meeting.

Overnight, the weather had deteriorated and below the now heavy grey sky the sea rose and fell to a long swell which would make the transfer of mail difficult; probably the first signs of a seasonal storm coming up from the south.

On Challenger's bridge, they watched Anzac approaching from astern, her bow lifting and falling twenty feet to the swell. In this weather, the manoeuvre would demand close attention to the positioning of the ships, relative to each other.

"Keep her steady as you can, Taffy. Nothing to starboard."

At slightly higher speed, Anzac drew alongside Challenger who, maintaining a steady fifteen knots and a ruler-straight course, was prepared to receive the mail from the other ship. Amidships, the short jackstay mast was in place, ready to receive the transfer line from the Australian.

The suction effect of the water, funnelling between the two ships, drew the two hulls closer together than either captain had intended and the Australian allowed his ship to fall back astern of Challenger so that he could try again. In Challenger, Commander Powers frowned; the First Lieutenant had come up to the bridge to supervise the transfer, toughing his cap in salute as their eyes met.

"He's making hard work of this Number One. I think we might be well advised to put a collision mat over the side?"

"Surely he won't come that close Sir."

He reached for the loud hailer microphone and pointed the bullhorn style speaker aft to speak to the seamen on the weather deck below, waiting to receive the lightweight Costain line from the other ship.

"Petty Officer Brown. Have a collision mat put over the side." The Petty Officer waved his hand in acknowledgement and understanding and four seamen lifted the lid of the adjacent weather deck locker and extracted the big, coir mat; suspending it over the ship's side to protect the hull should the two ships scrape together.

Petty Officer Brown's Australian opposite number, rifle in hand, waited for his opportunity to shoot the line attached to a short brass rod, across the gap between the ships; a bit like a Red Indian shooting a flaming arrow into the settler's wagon in a cowboy film.

Caught by the seamen waiting in Challenger, this line would be rove through the block attached to Challenger's jackstay mast and the heavier, carrier line hauled across and made fast. Petty Officer brown smiled to himself, piece of cake, done it hundreds of times. The mailbag could then be transferred and, the procedure reversed, the two ships would separate; Anzac to take up the inshore patrol and Challenger to seaward; on call but further from the enemy's guns. The ship's company could then stand down to cruising stations, eat and read their letters from home.

Anzac's pale grey painted prow, towering over the lower level of the Challenger's weather deck amidships, swept closer. Standing there watching, Brown could see that the Anzac's Captain, realising the danger they were in, was trying to fall astern again and at the same time swing her bow away.

"Too late, you Aussie prat!" Petty Officer Brown's comment was lost on the wind. There was no time to move the collision mat! Anzac's steel prow, caught by the attraction of the sea funnelling between the two ships and lifted by the swell, continued to swing inwards towards Challenger and the watching seamen.

"Other side, quick, lads." Brown had no intention of being standing there when the other ship hit them; he'd been in the navy too long to risk his life for a bag of letters; even if one of them might be for him.

Anzac's overhanging prow scraped down the after end of Challenger's starboard side, sweeping away the guardrails. Mesmerised, everyone listened to the scream of tearing metal as the longitudinal seam between Challenger's side plates and her weather deck was opened up, allowing the disturbed water compressed between the two ships to flood into the messdeck below.

Anzac was, by then, falling back, missing Challenger's starboard screw by only a few feet. The other ship's bow, dented but not seriously damaged, fell away astern.

"Signal from Anzac, Sir," Yeoman Houser reported to the Captain. "Whoops!"

* * *

The heavily mirrored wall at the back of the bar made an excellent sounding board and the words of the song could be heard clearly above the general hubbub.

21

The singer drew himself up to his full five foot six inches and projected the words, scanned to the tune of My Bonnie Lies Over The Ocean, in the fine, clear, Welsh tenor for which he had been famed amongst the congregation at his local church before taking the King's shilling and the Admiralty's Instructions.

> *Oh we are the Far East's destroyers*
> *We'll go to wherever we're bid*
> *We don't give a damn where they send us*
> *and They wouldn't care if we did!*

Other, less melodious voices took up the chorus.

> *Sea time its sea time*
> *That's what we're all destined to do, to do*
> *Sea time more sea time*
> *But we'll someday get back home to you.*

The singer pressed on, totally unconcerned that he was supported only by those few others in the bar that were from his own ship. Tonight, apart from the dozen or so members of the Challenger's ships company, the bar was filled to capacity with sailors from other, bigger ships; ships that spent less time at sea than did the destroyers and frigates.

He didn't like big ships. Big ships had too many officers and then there were the Royal Marines who acted as ship's policemen, he would rather put up with the extra sea time and the hardships in the little ships than all the regimentation in big ships. Big ships was like being in the army.

Challenger was in the dockyard for the repairs made necessary not by enemy action about which they could have boasted but by the Australian destroyer. The result of their fouled-up manoeuvre, a ten foot gash along the upper deck and the ship's starboard side had been filled by the relocated collision mat, with lashed up hammocks and reinforced by timber shoring to keep out the sea until Challenger could get back to Kure and that dockyard's ship repair facilities. To her ship's company, any excuse to be ashore in a bar was good enough.

In addition to the official reprimand issued by the Flotilla Leader, Captain 'D8' in Cossack, Commander Powers, had also had one or two well-chosen words to say to Anzac's captain. These had been reported throughout the ship as having largely to do with Sunday drivers and Aussies being a danger to navigation. Anzac's response, though not clearly audible aboard Challenger, was generally accepted to have made reference to whinging and ungrateful Pomes.

Someone put another bottle of beer in front of the singer who, thus encouraged, launched into the last verse and his shipmates joined in to help him drown out the rude comments from the other drinkers.

> *So, if you are a jolly good fellow*
> *'twill be Singapore for your next trip*
> *where the fleshpots will ruin your liver*
> *and the dockyard will ruin your ship.*

Some of the big-ship drinkers joined in the last chorus good humouredly and the singer emptied the bottle and rejoined his mates at their table.

"What d'yer reckon Hookey?" he asked.

Able Seaman Arthur was particularly keen to know where they were going next and for how long. He had served two years in Challenger and was looking forward to going home.

"Don't know mate," the Leading Seaman told him." I haven't heard anything you haven't heard."

"Yeah but you're mates with that Sparker who's a towny of your'n. I bet he knows; they know all the buzzes, stands to reason, they have to tell the skipper don't they."

"Well he hasn't told me anything so I can't help mate. Anyway, you've got another six months to go yet; foreign commissions are two and a half years, not two."

"Yeah but I don't want to be told in six months time, can't go home without relief and no reliefs available, do I?"

"I'm sure there's a long list of volunteers just waiting to get a chance to come out here and win a medal or two. All those barrack stanchions, lolling about in Chatham all day and going home to their wives every night. Embarrassed they are, all that doing nothing all day and collecting their living ashore allowance, their marriage allowance, their Government children's allowance and their civvy ration allowances; stands to reason, don't it. Nobody in their right mind would want to do that when they could be out here getting their balls shot off."

"Thanks for nothing Hooky."

"Sorry mate, I really don't know anything. "

"Can't you ask your towny?"

Leading Seaman Booker drained his glass and replaced it on the table. "No I fucking can't! If he hears anything he'll probably tell me and then, I'll tell you but I ain't asking; he'd never tell me anything again. Just because we come from the same town, doesn't mean we're blood brothers or something."

"Yeah Geof. I s'pose you're right. Its just that I don't want to dip out and miss my transfer home."

"Have a word with the ship's office Writer. He may know if a relief's been applied for and if not, he may be able to jog Jimmy the One's memory."

"Yeah, thanks, that a good idea. Want another beer?"

"No ta. I've had enough to float the Challenger out of dry dock tomorrow. Maybe they'll tell us something then, eh?"

TWO

The tug took the strain and Challenger was slowly drawn, stern first out of the re-flooded dry dock in which she had also taken advantage of the opportunity to check a weeping gland on the starboard shaft.

The repairs to her damaged side could almost as easily have been made good whilst afloat but the dry dock was there, it was empty, the gland had been giving trouble for some time and the opportunity to repack it properly was too good to miss.

Clear of the dock, the ship's own engines took over from the tug and, with a little help from the obliging tug master, Challenger docked alongside; once more whole and her own master.

"OK Number One, you may carry on with replenishment. I'll be in my day cabin if you need me. I have an appointment with the admiral this afternoon but until then, we don't actually belong to anybody, OK?"

Lieutenant Harry Enders, the First Lieutenant, acknowledged his captain's instruction and turned to the voice pipe. "Wheelhouse; Coxswain, finished with main engines. Pipe Foc'sle party and Special Sea Dutymen fall out. Replenishment parties to muster in the waist."

In his day cabin, Commander David Powers threw his hat on the desk and slumped into the chair. His steward appeared, as if by magic, in the doorway. "Anything I can get you Sir?"

"The elixir of youth would be nice but failing that, a large G&T would do very well."

He was not looking forward to the afternoon's meeting with the Admiral. Another three weeks patrolling off the west coast of Korea would be the almost inevitable outcome of the meeting, especially now that he had repacked the starboard shaft gland and had reported that it was no longer leaking. He would be, when replenishment was completed this afternoon, in all respects ready for sea, he could see no way of avoiding the boredom of another patrol.

His Steward placed a very large G&T on the desk. "Lunch, Sir?"

"Yes. In half an hour, say?"

Two parties of men were working on the upper deck. On the port side, a chain of men crossed and recrossed the gangway from the wharf carrying boxes and sacks of fresh, frozen and canned food and all the other stores needed by a ship expected to be at sea for at least a month and very possibly a great deal longer.

On the starboard side, another working party hefted ammunition from the barge moored alongside, passing it to the ammunition hoists that, this time, were lowering the shells and cartridges into the magazines rather than lifting them up to the guns. Normally a happy ship, this morning the Challengers were anything but that; storing and ammunitioning ship represented hard manual labour, not an activity to which sailors take naturally and this morning, it was raining.

At the starboard yardarm the red flag Baker, warning all other ships that she was handling explosives hung limp and sodden against its halyard; every so often, an equally wet signalman would shake it clear so that there could be no doubt what flag it was. For all that, the weather in Japan was better than it was at sea off the west coast of Korea.

The 4.5 inch shells being passed along the upper deck and in through the screen door to the ammunition hoists in the for'ard Petty Officer's mess weighed over forty pounds each. Whilst dropping one would not result in an explosion, the certain damage to any toe it landed on was guaranteed to keep the working party's minds on the job in hand. It would be easier this afternoon; by then the shells would all be inboard and they would be loading the much lighter brass cordite cartridges that would, when fired, propel the shells towards their target.

"Whatever you do, Nobby, don't drop one."

"Why not, Hooky? They won't explode if I do."

Leading Seaman Foster smiled at him, "No, Able Seaman Clark, it won't but the Chief Gunner will and I don't want to be the one in charge if that happens."

There was very little risk of anybody dropping a shell but the navy runs on banter and a little good-natured joshing by the Leading Hand in charge of the working party would ensure that nothing more serious occurred.

"How many more of these are we expected to hump, Hooky? It'll be dinner time soon."

"About as many as they can stow down below son. Now stop fucking about and get on with it, you're holding up the line."

Nobby's shell followed the previous one and was placed in the hoist where the man on the handle wound it bottom first down the chute into the magazine that served 'A' and 'B' guns, the for'ard main armament. In the for'ard magazine, three decks below, another working party transferred the shells from the hoist to the storage racks. Down here it was hot, sweaty work and it was always possible, with sweaty hands, to drop one. Each man had a sweat rag loosely tied round his neck and would wipe his hands every so often without being conscious of doing so. After a while, they became automatons;

lift and stow, lift and stow; time ceased to exist, the supply of ammunition coming down from the upper deck was endless.

"Come on, you lot. We want to get this lot stowed before the after working party finishes or they'll probably drink our tots." Abaft the gangway another working party was passing shells aft from the lighter to the magazines below 'X' and 'Y' guns and, as always in the service, there was fierce though friendly rivalry between the two working parties.

The port side working party were equally busy transferring boxes and sacks from the two lorries on the wharf to the relevant stores down below, The meat was being stowed in the refrigerated compartment together with butter and all the other things that needed to be kept refrigerated; fresh vegetables were being stowed in upper deck, steel mesh lockers where the fresh air, not to mention the salt spray, would help to keep them fresh for as long as possible. When they were exhausted, it would be back to the tins of peas, beans, potatoes, carrots, mixed diced vegetables, the ever present plum tomatoes and eventually, the dreaded powdered potato; all the things that the ship needed to remain at sea for months at a time.

Wax coated eggs, supposedly longer lasting than fresh ones, were stowed down below in the 'fridge together with as much fresh milk as was practical; after that, it would be back to the tins of evaporated milk again; why did they call it Ideal when, clearly, it wasn't?

The First Lieutenant knocked on the doorframe of the captain's cabin. "All 4.5 shells are inboard, Sir. The dockyard asks can they send the oiler alongside before the cordite so that it can go and fuel the Jamaica this afternoon?"

"Will it interfere with your plans, Number One?"

"No Sir and I've checked with the Chief and he's happy."

"OK, tell them to get on with it, I want to be ready to go

when the admiral tells me what he wants us to do and where he wants us to do it."

"Any chance of a change of scene, do you think, Sir? The east coast, perhaps?"

"Doubt it Harry, the Yanks seem to want to keep that more or less to themselves and want us to do the west coast. That way, I suspect, their war correspondents can be shown that they are doing it all by themselves, like last time."

"Ah well, Sir, it doesn't make a lot of difference, I suppose. Just that I reckon I know the west coast like the back of my hand and thought a change would be as good as a rest."

"You could always try prayer, Harry. Never worked for me but you could get lucky."

" I'll have a word with the Padre next time I see him Sir. Nothing ventured nothing gained, as they say."

The captain's steward silently laid up the table for lunch; the First Lieutenant's little joke would be all round the ship by that afternoon.

"How's the stores coming along?"

"Should be finished by midday. It'll be nice to have some fresh veggies for a while, eh Sir."

"Yes."

Through the open scuttle, they heard the ammunition lighter's lines being let go and the tug's whistle as she pulled the lighter away from the ship's side; on the flag deck, at the back of the bridge, the signalman lowered the red ammunitioning flag and stowed it in the flag locker ready for rehoisting this afternoon.

"I'd better go and confirm that the oiler is expected."

"Yes, carry on Number One."

"Do'y'hear there." The shrill whistle of the bosun's call attracted attention throughout the ship "Up spirits Hands to dinner."

Someone outside the open scuttle of the Captain's cabin completed the announcement, "Officers to lunch."

In the for'ard seamen's mess, the dismissed working parties were drinking their tots and the cooks of the mess were setting out the food on the long tables "Oh goody! Corned beef again. I hate corned beef."

"Well, at least the spuds are real ones, fresh onboard this morning they were Hookey. Anyway, you set the menu so you knew it would be corned beef again."

"That doesn't mean I have to like it."

As in all the navy's small ships, Challenger's catering arrangement was that known as canteen messing. In this system, the individual messes decided what they would be eating each day, would draw the appropriate stores and prepare the food for delivery to the galley for cooking. This allowed the mess caterer to buy private stores ashore if the mess was prepared to pay for them but even under such a relatively beneficial system, there was little real choice. Still, supper tonight was roast chicken and all the trimmings; that would make up for the corned dog.

Canteen messing was the norm in the destroyers. Only the bigger ships, the cruisers and carriers and the battleships, when there were any, luxuriated in professionally prepared food but none of the small ship men would swap ships for that. No, the atmosphere was better in the little ships, no Royal Marines to police the ship and only just enough officers and men to run it. In the small ships, everyone knew their job and could be relied upon to do it. No shirkers, no passengers and, therefore, very seldom any trouble.

Alongside, the car provided by the occupying Australian army pulled up at the gangway and the Captain was piped ashore. The admiral's satellite office in Kure was at the other end of the dockyard.

"Afternoon Powers." The admiral indicated a chair and placing his cap on the table by the door, Commander Powers sat. "We have a slight problem down south. It seems that some merchant skipper is having a bit of trouble with what he reports as a Nationalist Chinese heavy cruiser. Now, you know and I know that they haven't any heavy cruisers but that's why I asked for the oiler to sort you out first, David. I want you out of here by tonight, I want you to go and see what you can do about this, OK?"

"Of course, Sir. It would probably be a diplomatic mistake to actually open fire on the Nationalist Chinese navy's ship, we'd probably have politicians poking into every nook and cranny out here. Best if they remain in ignorance of just what we're doing, eh Sir?"

"Too true David, perish the thought. No. I want it sorted and I don't want either our merchant ship nor their warship, whatever it is, damaged; is that clear?"

"A touch of Nelsonian myopia, eh Sir."

"Exactly David. I want the right result and I don't want to know how you propose attaining it. Similarly, I don't want a host of bureaucrats descending on my office with clip-boards, wanting to know who did what to whom and for why. I want you to apply your well known special ability for convincing the enemy that they don't really want to fight."

"A detached operation 'll make a nice change Sir. To be absolutely honest, we're getting a bit bored with the Korean coast. I take it I am allowed to proceed at rather more than the economical cruising speed so beloved of our lords and masters at the Admiralty?"

"Go as fast as you like David and not too many messages in plain language eh? Don't want our American cousins to know too much about our business do we?"

David Powers grinned. Close co-operation was one thing, letting the Yanks know everything was quite another.

31

"Oh, and David. I may have another little jaunt for you when you get back. Not fixed yet but could be right up your street. A bit more intellectually demanding I should think."

THREE

Whilst, the further south they went, the warmer it got, the weather did them no favours. When it wasn't raining, it was blowing and when it was doing neither of these singly, it was probably doing both. At least, when it was only blowing, the sun shone and they felt better.

It being sunny and dry, the ship's open bridge was well populated. The captain sat in his sea chair with the first lieutenant standing beside him; neither of them concerned with the immediate operation of the ship. Yeoman Houser, though quite happy with the ability of the Leading Signalman of the watch Buster Hawkins to handle anything that might occur, had also come out of hiding to take the sun.

"Wonder why they couldn't send someone up from Hong Kong Sir, its much closer than we were?"

"Perhaps they haven't got anyone down there that's up to the job Number One. Facing a Nationalist heavy cruiser is no job for a sloop, is it? For that you need something big and strong like us!"

"But we know it isn't a heavy cruiser, Sir."

"I know that Number One and you know that and the Nationalist Chinese Navy knows that but it's a matter of face, you see. They couldn't possibly back down to a sloop, suppose we'd sent the Alert up there;

God, she's only got one bloody gun; she isn't going to frighten anyone. There's no way a Nationalist warship, whatever she is, is going to submit to her."

"No Harry, it's clearly a job for Superboat and at the moment, that's you, me and this worn out old destroyer; at least we still have our guns and torpedoes and we look like a warship. Anyway, I imagine that our adversary, if she is still there when we arrive, will be one of those old American destroyers that they gave the Nationalists a couple of years ago. They're supposed to be to defend the Formosa Strait against the Communist gunboats; even we're a good match for one of those."

Lieutenant Darling withdrew his head from the bridge chart table, under the forebridge canopy and straightened his back. "Either I'm getting taller or that damned table is getting lower down. My back's killing me."

"So, Pilot, do you know where we are?"

"Yes, Sir. We are in 25 degrees 15 minutes North, 127 degrees 40 minutes East We've got about 200 miles to go before turning north round Iriomote-jima into the East China Sea and passing Chilung into the Formosa Strait from the north or roughly five hundred miles if you want to loop south around Formosa and into the Strait by Kaohsiung."

"Where's this damned merchant ship, what's it called?"

"She's the City of Canterbury Sir. She's hove too off Xiamen."

"Right, we'd better go on and swing round the bottom of Formosa, that will give the nationalist less warning that we are coming to her assistance; we don't want to precipitate anything unpleasant before we're ready to do something about it. What's our ETA off T'ainan?"

"Two o-clock tomorrow afternoon, Sir."

"That won't do. OK, Chas," he turned to Lieutenant Turner the officer of the watch, "I think we should wind her up to thirty knots. What time will that get us there Pilot?"

"About two in the morning Sir."

"I like that much better, gives us the element of surprise."

"Not if their radar is any good, Sir."

"They'll almost certainly have it on short range, looking out for Communist gunboats, we should be able to sneak up from the south east without disturbing them. OK Chas? Thirty knots please. Do we want the same course Pilot?"

"Yes please Sir, 195 until quite late tonight. I don't suppose it matters Sir, but we are about to cross the tropic of Cancer."

"You're right Pilot, it doesn't matter but you can tell the troops that if you then want to explain why you've done so."

The officer of the watch bent over the voice pipe. "Wheelhouse. 290 revolutions."

The telegraphsman in the wheelhouse rang on 290 revs and the repeater from the engineroom repeated it back. The quartermaster on the wheel lifted his head to speak into the big brass trumpet-end of the voice pipe. "Two Niner Zero revolutions showing Sir."

"Thank you. 290 revolutions repeated Sir."

* * *

The Formosa Strait, formed by the island of Formosa standing offshore from the Chinese mainland, connects the South China Sea to the East China Sea and eventually, to the Yellow Sea.

Formosa itself forms one of the major islands in a line joining Japan to the Philippines to the east of which, the Pacific ocean extends uninterrupted to the west coast of America.

Inside this natural offshore barrier, the seas are shallow and not to be treated lightly in the typhoon season, the word typhoon being a corruption of the old Chinese term tai fung or, great wind The ancients used this otherwise easily navigable route from China to the Philippines and Indonesia to establish a flourishing trading empire.

Now, two or more thousand years later, the captain of the City of Canterbury stood on the starboard flying bridge watching the Chinese warship. He had ignored the warship's order to return to Hong Kong but had agreed to heave to under the other's guns.

The signal sent to the Company's agent in Hong Kong two days ago had made the position clear. He was, to all intents and purposes under arrest but not as yet, actually incarcerated. He had not been boarded, neither had he lowered his flag in submission; it was as if the Nationalists were simply waiting for him to give up and go home.

He turned to his first officer, standing beside him. "Well Jim, what do we do now?"

"If I remember the advice of one of my commanding officers during the war, I recommend that we continue following a course of masterly inaction."

"You were RNR weren't you? Destroyers"

"Only briefly Sir. Most of the time we RNR temporary gentlemen were privileged to be given command of corvettes or, if lucky, perhaps a sloop; destroyers were for the professional sailors, Royal Navy officers with a career to maintain."

"Well some of it seems to have rubbed off on you, you're probably right. Of course we could simply sail back to Honkers, in which case I imagine he will leave us alone or we could set course for Xiamen but in that case I have the feeling that he could become aggressive. We shall just have to wait for advice from the owners; I suppose you are certain that the agent did acknowledge our signal?"

"Oh yes, Sir. I made damn sure of that. Demanded a real, a proper acknowledgement. It's on the file and entered in the log."

"The RN must have taught you something then, Jim. You've got to give them credit for that. It's a great comfort to have the security of a real belt and braces man as my First."

"I learned that as a Cadet, Sir. Long before taking the King's shilling."

"What do you reckon she is? All I can see is her superstructure."

"Massive so, presumably she's a cruiser at least. Don't understand why she hasn't come in any closer to inspect us."

"Well, presumably, if she is a cruiser, she will have six or even eight inch guns and can reach us very well from there. Perhaps she doesn't think it necessary to come any closer. Perhaps, she is worried about there being bigger guns than hers on shore just behind us, waiting for her to come in close enough for them to have a go at her?"

"Now that's an idea Jim. Suppose we allow ourselves to drift slowly towards the shore. Not directly towards Xiamen, that would be foolhardy but just a little closer under the protection of any guns that may be there. The authorities ashore will know who we are and why we're here so, with anything like reasonable luck they won't shoot at us but it might just discourage our friend out there a little. Increase the range a little. Frankly I don't like sitting here waiting for him to make his mind up what he is going to do. Clearly we can't just sit here indefinitely and just as clearly, he ain't going to let us proceed so it's a stalemate."

"If it's chess he wants to play, Sir, how about a feint towards Xiamen, see what he does about it, this could all be a bluff."

"You are suggesting that I put my ship into danger, hazard my command just to see if that bugger sinks us?"

"To be perfectly honest Sir, I don't think he would dare but on the other hand, I can't be sure of that. Trigger happy, some of these guys, now that they have their new toys like that one out there."

"You could be right but I don't think I'll risk upsetting them any more than I must. We'll just drift back a bit in the general direction of the shore and ever so slightly towards Xiamen, OK?"

The First Officer walked into the bridge and ordered

minimum revs astern. It would be some time before the warship noticed anything had changed and by then, they would be a little closer to shore and also to their intended port of call.

It was perfectly safe to continue with this manoeuvre for about an hour before they needed to concern themselves with shallowing water. At this rate, of about two or three knots, they could probably put another two miles between themselves and their adversary before they noticed anything. Even two miles on the range might help if push came to shove.

Captain Mellows nodded to him as he returned to the wing "OK Sir. We can ease back for about an hour without any hazard and with luck, they won't notice that we have increased the range."

"I hope you're right Jim. I had rather hoped that the war was over; this is supposed to be peacetime sailoring we're doing."

"I think that rather depends upon whose side you're on Sir. They are at war and we are comforting the enemy in their view. I'm not sure what that makes us but it probably doesn't make us bosom buddies."

"Who's got the watch?"

"Fourth Sir."

"Good, he's sound enough. Let's us go and get a drink, I feel the need coming on."

He stuck his head in through the door. "Fourth, I'll be in my cabin if we hear from either our friend over there or from our owners. I imagine that one or even perhaps both will want to talk to us sooner or later."

"Let's hope it's the owners who speak first, eh Sir?"

"It would make life easier, I agree."

"There's no danger of the owners telling us to proceed into harbour and damn the consequences, is there Sir?"

"Have you any idea what a ship like this costs? No owner

is going to risk losing her just to show bravado. Unless, of course, the Admiralty orders them to do so and guarantees to replace her should she be lost."

"Oh Sir! You don't think that's possible do you?"

"No Fourth, I don't but then again, who am I to second guess the owners? There is always the remote possibility that they might want a nice new ship and that we have been sent out here to get this one sunk so that they can claim on the insurance. It wouldn't be the first time that had happened."

Fourth Officer Bryant looked at his Captain, hoping to see a broad smile on his face but it wasn't there. "You're not serious are you Sir?"

"No lad but it has been known in the old days between the wars when trade was short and ships were cheap."

"But we're a modern ship Sir, well found and all that."

"You're right, of course Lad. Let me know if anything moves out there or anything comes in from the owners; OK?"

"Yes Sir."

"And, you'd better take bearings astern every fifteen minutes, just to make sure we don't bump into anything. Heave to in, say an hour unless you think it necessary before."

"What do you really think Sir? Are we being used as a dummy run to see what happens?" Mellows waved his First Officer to a chair and poured a large whiskey from the bottle standing in the rack on his desk.

"To be honest Jim, I have no idea, I was given no instructions by the owners. It is just possible that they didn't think the Nationalists would interfere with legitimate trade but then, from their point of view, it ain't legitimate. I'm afraid we shall just have to wait and see what happens. I don't suppose we are in any real danger but you might just check that everything is in order, just in case. Drink that first though."

* * *

Commander Powers, in Challenger, sat down to dinner satisfied that he had done all that he could to avoid early detection by Formosa. He was well out to sea and proceeding at great speed towards Hong Kong. He was well outside Formosa's claimed territorial waters so should cause them no alarm. He would be in a position, at about midnight, to slew round the southern tip of Formosa and make a dash for Xiamen and the City of Canterbury; assuming that she was still where she was last reported to be.

Presumably, if she wasn't, the owners would have reported that to CinC who would have told him. He certainly wasn't going to alarm the Formosan authorities by contacting the City of Canterbury directly. The Nationalist Chinese navy would be monitoring the usual commercial radio frequencies.

At thirty knots, the whole ship vibrated, shuddering like a wild thing. The two huge bronze screws, thrashing the water below were throwing up a wake that stood taller than her stern, building up a high wall of white water that followed the ship. If, for any reason, the ship should suddenly lose its forward momentum, a broken shaft perhaps, this wall of water could collapse on to the ship. It was for that reason that the pipe had been made that the quarterdeck was out of bounds to all but necessary hands.

For'ard, the destroyer's sharp bow cut through the water as it had been designed to do and threw out a bow wave on either side of the foc's'le in a most impressive manner. For those within the foc's'le, in the seamen's mess decks, life was rather less comfortable than for the officers who were sitting at table in the wardroom one deck above them and a little further aft; they, being at the relative centre of gravity of the ship, sat in comparative comfort. Only the captain's cabin was marginally more comfortable.

The men in the after messdeck would have no chance of any comfort through the night. Their mess would be thundering through the water with the twin shafts spinning immediately below them and the screws only a few feet further aft. The vibration on the after mess deck would make sleep impossible. The more savvy amongst them had already collected their hammocks and emigrated for'ard to beg space in one of the other messes. There wouldn't be any spare hammock slingings but they could doss down on the deck under the mess tables or anywhere else they could find a little space. Bad as it would be, it would be more comfortable than staying down aft. As long as they made sure that they could be found when it was their watch on deck, no one would interfere with this totally unofficial arrangement.

Commander Powers sat in his sea chair on the bridge. It was twelve thirty and the Navigator was checking his position. "Any time now, Sir. We need a course of 270 for about an hour and then round to 330 for about another hour. We then need 000 to bring us up to a position between where we think the City of Canterbury is and the supposed position of the Nationalist warship. We should be in position at about dawn Sir, God willing. Should be able to see what we're doing. Radar will of course tell us what's going on, if anything."

"You know, Pilot, I never cease to be amazed by your confidence. When I was your age, I would have made at least most of that a suggestion to my captain rather than a list of instructions."

"Was that in the days of sail, Sir?"

"I think you have shown enough self confidence for one night Pilot, don't push your luck. OK Guns, take her round as Pilot has instructed, let me know when you have settled on 270. No need to call me when you alter to 330 but call me when you turn on to 000, OK?"

"Very good Sir."

He slid down the handrails of the ladder, down to his sea cabin, enjoying the feeling of speed and noticing that his knees didn't absorb the shock of landing quite the way they had when he was a young midshipman. Ah well, he was now a senior Commander and shouldn't be sliding down handrails like that anymore. Made him feel good though; a moment's resurgence of youth. You never knew, they might be going into action tomorrow morning against another warship, possibly an equal battle and it would have been a pity not to have taken the opportunity. Eat, drink and be merry for tomorrow we may die. Nonsense!

In his cabin, he sat at his desk and read the letter to Sable that he had begun yesterday. No hurry to finish it, nowhere to post it until they got back to Kure. It seemed strange to have someone to write to again, somehow it gave you a feeling of belonging, of having another life outside the ship and duty.

FOUR

"What do you think they're up to Sir?"

"Who Flags?"

"The Admiralty Sir. They must know that the Nationalists have instituted a blockade of the mainland Chinese ports anywhere near Formosa. Well, actually they have announced a blockade of all Chinese ports but they're only in a position to enforce it against the few ports close to Formosa itself. I don't understand why the Admiralty should tell us to assist this merchant ship that's trying to run the blockade. None of our business really, is it Sir?"

"Alas, Flags, when the Admiralty tells us to do something, it behoves us to consider it to be some of our business. That's the way the navy works; or hadn't you noticed?"

"Oh, I didn't mean that Sir. What I meant was, why do they want this merchant ship to break the blockade?"

Admiral Dickenson's new, shore-side office was furnished comfortably at last with a couple of easy chairs and a low, occasional table in front of the open, metal fly-screened window; these had been placed far enough from his desk to suggest that this was a suite rather than just an over large, one room, temporary office.

For some months, Rear Admiral Aubrey Dickenson, FO2 Far East, had been fighting a lengthy battle with various junior but determined officers to obtain what he regarded as the minimum comforts necessary for him to receive visitors to

43

his office. He had finally managed to explain to the appropriate Supply Captain that, as the local British CinC, he must have an office suite at least as comfortable as that boasted by his American equivalent. And, that that office must be ashore, not afloat on the old, borrowed, Yangtse steamer temporarily renamed HMS Ladybird! National shame had finally got him the few small comforts that authority had not been able to obtain.

The two officers sat companionably, glass in hand, watching the sun set outside. It had been a long day and it had become the custom for Admiral Dickenson at this time to dispense with the appearances of the authority vested in him and to invite his Flag Lieutenant to join him in a pre-evening drink. Later, at some function or other, or in company with other officers, they would revert to master and servant status but just for this few minutes, whenever possible, the Admiral liked to acknowledge if only to himself that the Flag Lieutenant was also the son of his mistress; a coincidence not widely known within the service and certainly not known to the young man.

Just what his reaction would have been, had he known that his mother had for many years been the mistress of Aubrey Dickenson the Admiral would probably never know but the Admiral hoped that he would have been pleased that his widowed mother had found happiness after the death of his father during the war.

"I imagine that My Lords, Commissioners of the Admiralty have very little to do with it my boy." He sipped his gin and tonic, shaking the ice in the glass. "I don't know, of course, such people like to work on the principle of not letting the right hand know what the left hand is doing but I suspect that the politicians have something to do with it."

"Sorry Sir?"

"The damned Government Boy! Who the Hell is in government at home?"

"The Labour Party Sir."

"Precisely, the Socialists. And. whose is the de-facto government of China now that Chiang Kai-shek's lot has been driven out?"

"The communists Sir."

"Got it in one, eh? I suspect that the temptation for the government to form some unofficial alliance with their fellow socialists in China would be backed by the none-too-fastidious element in the Board of Trade and a small-scale trial of strength is in progress.

"If the Nationalist Chinese in Formosa forcibly restrain our merchant ship from entering some totally unimportant small port on the Chinese mainland, an international incident would ensue. Lots of diplomatic or probably less than diplomatic messages passed back and forth between us and the Nationalist Chinese and both sending copies to the United Nations.

"On the other hand, if they chicken out of actually arresting or sinking our merchant ship to prevent her entering the port, then the blockade is shown to be nothing more than an announcement, a puff of hot air. Interesting, eh?"

"But what if they do arrest her or even, God forbid, sink her?"

"Ah, that's where we come into the equation or rather, the ever faithful Challenger. She is, you will recall at this very moment on her way to stand by our gallant merchant captain who is, one is assured, only trying to carry out the lawful instructions of his owners. Instructions that must I suspect, have been sanctioned by the Board of Trade on behalf of the British Government."

"I hope Powers has enough sense not to actually start another war down there, we have our hands rather full up here at the moment and I have an appointment in Tokyo with General MacArthur tomorrow which, I suspect, means that he wants something more from us."

"You might sort out the present disposition of ships for the morning, I shall probably have to explain why we can't be expected to do any more than we're doing; whilst having a perfectly workable plan for doing just that should he suggest something sensible."

"Of course, Sir." He placed his empty glass on the table and stood, collected his cap from the small table beside the door and left.

Admiral Dickenson remained where he was, looking out of the window, watching the shadows lengthen and finally disappear as the sun fell behind the workshops and stores buildings on the opposite side of the basin.

His relationship with his wife had been more dynastic that romantic ever since they had been introduced by her father who had, he claimed later, spotted the young Lieutenant's potential both as a naval officer and as a potential husband for his younger daughter.

Her riding accident as a child had left her with a slight but noticeable limp resulting in a less than satisfactory ability to dance and a rather uninviting scar on her left cheek. Not, one would have thought, an unovercomable social disadvantage, modern cosmetics being what they are. The problem with service marriages is that, being super fit themselves, the suitable young men tended to expect the same degree of Adonis-like stature in their wives; certainly at the time of the marriage.

Aubrey Dickenson had made no serious objection to being placed next to his Admiral's daughter at various functions and later, at private dinner parties. Over a period of a few years, it had become recognised that they were an item; that he was to be the admiral's son in law.

He had to admit that this arrangement had not been too onerous. The girl was pleasant enough, if a little undersexed as a result of her convent schooling and he did like her a great deal. She had proved a good wife but had been unable to become a mother and slowly their relationship had settled into a kind of genuine if loveless friendship. Thank God he couldn't do the same thing to his Flag Lieutenant; he had no daughter to wish upon him.

He drained his glass and placed it beside the other on the table. Side by side, friends, like the two men. As he had been with the boy's father before he had gone down in Hood.

That was how it had started of course. He had gone to see her, to offer what comfort he could in the circumstances. She had been brave, accepted that, in war, sailors got killed, she just didn't see why it had had to be her sailor. God, was that really ten years ago. He must write to her. Tell her how the boy was doing.

His secretary heard him leave, cleared the glasses, turned off the light and closed the door of his office. Second Officer Wren Daphne Archer was fond of her Admiral but fonder of Lieutenant Terrence, Terry Bowden, his Flag Lieutenant; she was pleased that her two favourite men were friends as well as colleagues.

In his own office next door, Lieutenant Bowden made up a file for the Admiral's tomorrow meeting with General Douglas MacArthur, Supreme Commander, United Nations Forces, Korea. MacArthur had a reputation for expecting his Heads of Department, and that included Limey Admirals, to be properly briefed and to be able to keep up with his own quickness of mind. He expected them to be on top of their job and, if there was anything he could do to ensure that his Admiral confirmed in MacArthur this opinion, he would willingly stay up all night.

"If you don't need me Sir, I'll be off home."

He looked up at the interruption. Second Officer Archer stood in the doorway, the light in the corridor behind her throwing her neat, uniformed figure into silhouette. He smiled at her. "No Daphne, I can manage. Off you go. Don't pick up any strange sailors on your way home, eh?"

"I don't do strange, Sir. I like my men plain and simple.

"I'll remember that. Good night."

"Good night." She omitted the terminal Sir

In the new darkness outside, Second Officer Daphne Archer strolled slowly towards the point along the wharf from which the pinnace would ferry her out to the safety and rather utility comfort of her accommodation on the Head Quarters ship anchored out in the bay.

In his office, making sure that his Admiral had everything he could possibly need for the morrow, Lieutenant Terry Bowden's thoughts wandered sufficiently off course to conjure up a mental picture of Second Officer Archer without her uniform. Not naked. No, not naked but in civilian clothes, a pretty dress, the sort of dress one might wear to a ball.

He wondered if she had ever been to a hunt ball? In many ways they were a crashing bore but they did provide an annual means of introducing a new girl to one's friends. To signal to all and sundry that you and she were henceforth to be considered an item; though not, one hoped, the subject of gossip.

He pushed the thought from his mind. They hardly knew each other, damn it they hadn't even been alone together outside the office but the thought was there, it would grow, he knew it would. He wondered what she thought of him, had she even thought of him at all other than as her Admiral's Flag Lieutenant?

He turned out the light and locked the door. Outside in the dark, he walked along the wharf towards the ferry steps, following the route she had taken earlier. It was ridiculous, they lived on the same ship, within a few yards of each other but they hadn't had any real social contact at all. He would do something about that; he would like to do something about that.

FIVE

The City of Canterbury's manoeuvre of apparently drifting slowly shorewards had not been followed by the warship who, it seemed, was content to just sit there waiting for the British ship to do something or go home.

"Well, I don't know Jim, I'm beginning to wonder whether our gallant owners are going to offer any advice at all. We can't just sit here indefinitely."

"Perhaps we should remind them that we're here, Sir? You know, send a signal asking about arrangements to replenish and refuel if they want us to remain here for more than a few more days."

"Somehow, I don't think that would go down too well at Head Office. These desk-bound sailors don't take kindly to sarcasm. No, we'll just have to wait a little longer but if we get no instructions by tomorrow lunchtime, I shall make course for Xiamen and see what happens."

"Suppose they shoot at us, Sir?"

"Then that is an act of war and the Admiralty cannot refuse to recognise it as such. We could be the cause of world war three Jim, just think of it, fame at last."

"Not a prospect that altogether pleases, Sir but I don't see what else we can do. We can't just sit here, it's ridiculous."

"There is, of course, another possible explanation for our apparent abandonment."

"Sir?"

"Our owners, in cahoots with the Government, have agreed that we should break the Nationalist's blockade of these ports and are waiting to see what the Nationalists are going to do about it. In that case, there ought to be a British warship loitering somewhere close by, like the US Seventh Cavalry in the cowboy movies, ready to come to our assistance should we actually be fired upon. All we have to do is pray that it gets here before we get into any serious trouble."

"Like being sunk?"

"I doubt if even that trigger happy lot would go that far but an unlucky shot could produce that undesired effect and I for one am in no hurry to be a dead hero. At midday, we ring on revolutions for ten knots and proceed to Xiamen, notifying our owners in plain language that we are doing so. That should produce some sort of a reaction."

"Probably by the Nationalist navy out there, Sir."

"Can you think of an alternative, other than doing nothing?"

"No Sir. Gung ho and all that then, eh?"

"As you say Jim, gung ho, though I don't think that's actually Chinese for anything."

"No Sir, it's Hollywood for up and at 'em, I think."

"Then, where's John Wayne when we need him?"

"Did you know that his real name is Marian, Sir?"

"Then that probably explains why he isn't here. Never mind Jim, I'm for turning in. Whose got the middle watch?"

"Third, Sir. I thought I should take the morning just in case there are any developments."

"Yes, probably a good idea. OK good night."

The pinkish grey light of the false dawn peaked above the horizon to the east for only a moment and was gone. In a few minutes, the true dawn would show a brightening horizon and life would begin again in a new day. It was funny how, however long you spent at sea and however many night watches you kept, the new dawn always seemed to lift the spirit and offer a new beginning; as someone had said, it was the beginning of the rest of your life. All that had gone before was past and couldn't be retrieved nor altered in any way. Today was the beginning of time and, tomorrow might never come.

Challenger steamed at a slightly reduced speed towards the position estimated by the Pilot, a position marked in pencil on the chart. At long-range setting, her radar had picked up an echo on the starboard bow, not very big but solid enough to be a proper ship rather than a large junk or something like that.

"Not big enough for a heavy cruiser, Sir."

"No Chas but big enough. What are the odds that she's an old USN destroyer, one of those they gave the Nationalists a couple of years ago?"

"Pretty safe bet, I would have thought, Sir. Not much else it could be; unless, of course, she isn't Nationalist but Communist."

"In that case she could be almost anything from an old Japanese cruiser downwards. Have to admit I have no idea just what they have or where they are. Have the hands fed and watered and closed up at defence stations by six, will you. Just in case."

The officer of the watch bent over the voice pipe. "Quartermaster. Call the hands. Hands to defence stations at 0600."

They could hear the pipe being broadcast through the ship's Tannoy PA system and could imagine the comments being made below in the mess decks. Never mind; if they couldn't take a joke, they shouldn't have joined.

The on watch Petty Officers could be heard moving through the ship making sure that the pipe was obeyed. "I'm up, every bugger's up Wakey Wakey you lot. The sun's burning your eyes out, hands off cocks, on socks!"

"Plot. Can you make out any other ships? Should be one about the same size to port, close in to shore I should think."

"Nothing showing Sir but there's a lot of clutter close in, reflected echoes from the land of course. "

"Keep an eye on it will you. I want to know where the other ship is before I make any positive move."

Commander Powers had been on the bridge since the alteration of course to 000 and was in need of coffee. "Messenger. Nip down to the wardroom and see if you can find some coffee. Three cups."

Able seaman Masters, the bridge messenger, knew from long experience that the captain took three sugars, the navigating officer one and Lt. Enders the first lieutenant and this morning the officer of the watch, took sweeteners. He hoped that the wardroom stewards were up and about.

"Bridge, Plot. Contact bearing red ten, extreme range but I'm pretty sure it's your merchant ship. Too big for one of their gunboats or junks."

"Thank you Plot. Keep an eye on it. I want to know if she's under way or anchored. I also want to know if there are any more contacts anywhere near her, small boats, that sort of thing. What's the warship doing?"

"Just sitting there, Sir. No apparent movement from either of them."

"There probably will be when they spot us. I'm surprised they haven't done so already. Must be keeping a bloody awful radar watch. Ah, Yeoman, Good morning." Yeoman Houser had reached the bridge and was checking with the Signalman of the watch that all was in order. "You 'd better stand by to be challenged by the ship bearing green two zero."

Yeoman Houser put the binoculars to his eyes and quickly spotted the dark silhouette of a large warship against the early morning light. "Keep your eyes on that young Martin. Any sign of anything, I want to know. OK?"

"Your every wish is my command Yeo."

"Never mind the repartee, keep your eyes on that ship."

Throughout the ship, the pipe was made, "Hands to Defence Stations."

"Well, here we go Number One. Who's relieving you as OOW?"

"Lt. Turner, Sir."

"Very good. Off you go."

Harry Enders handed over the watch to Chas Turner and disappeared below to the damage control centre from which he would keep everything under control in the event of action.

Powers leant forward and pressed the red button for the action stations klaxon. On the bridge, two more lookouts closed up at their positions, the Yeoman took over the watch from the signalman who remained as his second and from throughout the ship, reports began to come in. Guns crews closed up, gunnery director crew closed up. Torpedo tubes crew closed up, quarterdeck sentry closed up. Even the anti-submarine Squid mortar crew was closed up although there was no likelihood of a submarine engagement.

Lt. Turner reported to the Captain. "Ship at action stations, Sir."

"Thank you."

Captain Chin Wa, only recently made up to Captain and given command of Destroyer 375 – the gift of the US navy – peered over the shoulder of the radar operator, looking at the fast moving contact that had been reported.

"What do you reckon it is?"

"At that speed Sir, almost certainly a warship and, if it is, almost certainly British I would think."

Chin Wa recognised the intelligence of the operator and didn't choke him off for insolence as perhaps he would otherwise have done; this changed the entire situation.

He turned to his first Lieutenant who was standing behind him, also looking at the radar screen. "Inform base that a British warship has entered the Strait. Request instructions."

His instructions had been perfectly clear up until this point. The merchant ship was to be intimidated into turning round and sailing away from its supposed port of destination. Alternatively, she was to be stopped and cowed into remaining where she was until advised by her owners. Under no circumstances was the British merchant ship to be harmed; this was a diplomatic face-up not a war. The arrival of the British warship complicated matters and he wanted specific orders to deal with the changed situation.

Signalman Martin waited, his eyes firmly fixed on the Nationalist warship, waiting for a challenge. On the other side of the bridge, the port lookout watched the merchant ship, waiting for some sort of challenge or acknowledgement of their arrival.

"Not what you'd call awake, are they?"

Powers smiled. "Let's hope it stays that way, eh?"

"Challenge Sir," the Yeoman called out. "What ship?"

"Reply HMS Challenger. Good morning."

Signalman Martin clicked the Aldis lamp at the other ship.

"Reply acknowledged Sir."

"Now we wait and see what happens. Can you make her out Yeo? What do you reckon she is?"

"Bloody great tripod mast Sir and high superstructure, can't see anything else yet Sir. Yes I can. I know what she is. She's one of those old USN boats. You know the ones Sir, left over from World War One and modernised in '43 to form a training flotilla for the Yankee navy's recruits." "I'd know her anywhere, I was on one of the three they sold us in '42, bloody archaic she was. Couldn't knock the skin off a rice pudding. They had four four inch singles and a few heavy machine guns mounted abaft the funnel, torpedoes and a few depth charges. They had those big masts and high bridges to scare off the faint hearted I think."

"You think we are reasonably safe then?"

"Unless she's been modernised quite a bit since then, Sir."

"I'll take your word for it Yeoman, I think I can see her upper deck now and there doesn't seem to be much there to scare us off. Still, let's not be too confident. Chas, I think a turn to port to put us between the two ships, closer to the merchant ship if you please."

"Yeoman, see if you can raise someone on the merchant ship. I want to know their state."

A light flashed from the merchant ship, somewhat hesitantly at first but gaining in confidence by the third sentence. It was obviously some time since their operator, probably their wireless officer, had attempted to make Morse by light.

"Reports that all is well but that they're glad to see us. Please may they go into harbour now or, better still, go home?"

A flash of light from the Nationalist destroyer caught their eye and a waterspout leapt up from behind the merchant ship.

"Shit, she's opened fire on her. Guns, I want a shot just a little short of the warship bearing green five zero."

"'A' gun, ranging shot, green five zero elevation seven zero. Shoot."

The ding ding of the gun firing bell ensured that they were ready for the bang that followed. All eyes were on the other ship. It would be a pity if the shot went too close and did some damage but it had to go close enough to warn their adversary that, in a shooting match, they were on a hiding to nothing.

"Yeoman. Make to the warship. Cease fire or I shall be forced to engage. Then, to the merchant ship, carry out your owner's instructions."

Yeoman Houser pointed the starboard ten inch signal lamp

at the other warship and sent the message. The big signal lamp's beam in the still sunless morning light looked more like a lighthouse than a signal lamp. Martin using the smaller, four inch, Aldis lamp told the City of Canterbury to carry our her owner's instructions. Both reported that their signals had been acknowledged.

Another flash from the Nationalist warship's for'ard gun was seen less than a second before the projectile was heard passing over the automatically ducking heads of those on Challenger's bridge.

A second waterspout erupted, this time ahead of the merchant ship which, very sensibly; decided that a moving target would be harder to hit than a stationary one and kept moving, increasing speed steadily.

Powers sat. " I think we'll wait a moment and see if that was an act of bravado prior to submission or whether they really mean to start a war" Minutes passed with no further shooting.

"Bridge, Plot. Aircraft bearing green nine zero, three thousand feet."

"Ah, so that's it. They've decided on a show of force. Guns. Did you hear that?"

"Yes Sir; 'B' Gun, 'X' and 'Y' guns, train on bearing green nine zero, follow director. Load HE. Bofors train on bearing green nine zero angle of sight one one zero. 'A 'gun remain on bearing green five zero, load semi-armour piercing."

"Yeoman. Signal the warship. Call off your dogs and go home, you have made your point."

As he spoke, three Sabre jets screamed over the Challenger and towards the City of Canterbury, closer inshore. As they did so, anti-aircraft fire from the mainland shore erupted in front of them and they sheared off, turning for home but heading towards Challenger again on the way.

"Hold tight Guns, I don't think they mean to do us any harm."

He was right. The Sabres screamed low over the ship then climbed rapidly towards the east just as the sun appeared from behind the island of Formosa. "Very impressive, eh Chas? Now we wait and see."

"Signal from warship Sir. Port of Xiamen is closed."

"Reply. Thank you."

The Nationalist warship flashed the R to indicate that it had received the message.

"Plot, Bridge. Where's the merchant ship relative to Xiamen port."

"Another fifteen minutes and she'll be inside, Sir."

"Very well. Thank you. Yeoman. Make to the City of Canterbury. I think you are safe enough now. Good morning and good luck."

They watched as the merchant ship turned to port and disappeared behind a small island off the entrance of the port.

"Bridge, Plot. The warship is moving off to starboard Sir. No sign of any more aircraft."

"Thank you Plot. I think we have done our good deed for the day but keep an eye on her."

"Yeoman. Signal to FO2 FE. City of Canterbury has entered Xiamen. Chinese Nationalist warship appears to be returning to base. We shall do likewise when situation resolved. OK?"

"We'll remain at Action Stations for the present Chas, just in case."

"Bridge, Plot. Pilot, what course do I want for Sasebo?"

"Zero three zero, Sir."

"Thank you Pilot. Chas, I think we'll have course zero three zero, revolutions for fourteen knots. No need to rush back, I think."

"Zero three zero, Sir, one four eight revolutions." He repeated the order to the Coxswain in the wheelhouse below and acknowledged its repetition and confirmation.

"Course zero three zero, Sir, one four eight revolutions. Ship remains at Action Stations."

"Thank you. That will take us past the entrance to Xiamen, we'll take a gander inside if we can; might be worth knowing what's in there. Yeoman, why don't you have your young signalman nip up on top of the Director with your cruiserscope; see what he can see from up there?"

"Off you go Lad. Now's your chance to make a name for yourself." He handed him the big cruiser telescope which, held steady, would give a much better look than the binoculars on the bridge.

Not yet at the fourteen knots rung-on, the gunnery Director was stable enough for Martin to lay the big telescope across the top and to focus on the entrance to the tiny port.

"Not a lot to see, Sir. The Canterbury is being warped alongside and I can see a small coaster and, I think, two gunboats. Plenty of sampans, not much else, Sir.Lot of building work going on though Sir, I can see scaffolding."

"Thank you Signalman. I wonder why their gunboats didn't come out to escort the merchantman in? Not worth risking them, perhaps. Still, it tells us something about how much they value our merchant ship, doesn't it."

The Captain nodded to the Yeoman. "OK Martin, you can come down. Pass me that glass down before you drop it."

Martin resumed his position at the front of the bridge, starboard side, the position always occupied by the signalman of the watch and handy for the voice pipe down to the wireless office below.

"Right. In future lad, you'll be known as 'all my eye and Betty Martin' or, Betty for short, OK?"

"Whatever you say, Yeo."

The Officer of the Watch looked at the Yeoman. "Christ,

you must be much older than you look Yeoman if you remember that expression. It was a favourite of my father's."

"And mine, Sir."

"Bridge, Plot. Their warship appears to be hove to. No movement discernable."

"Thank you, Plot. Keep an eye on her though"

Captain Chin Wa read the signal handed to him by the messenger. He turned to his officer of the watch with a smile. "We are to break off the engagement and return to harbour." He handed the officer the signal, telling him to have it filed and left the bridge, going below to his cabin. Only when there did he allow the look of relief to show on his face. He had not been keen on the idea of starting a fire fight with the British destroyer; he was outclassed.

In Sasebo, Flag Lieutenant Bowden handed the signal to the Admiral. "Seems to have gone off quietly enough Sir. Have to admit I wasn't too sure what would happen. Suppose the Nationalists had done something silly?"

"Then Powers would have had to earn his Captain's pay by making a decision."

SIX

General Douglas MacArthur, U.S.Army, Supreme Commander United Nations Forces Korea, stood facing the assembled officers in the large office being used for the meeting. Around the table stood his fellow Americans, Admiral Joy USN, CinC Far East US Naval Forces, Joy's Chief of Staff, Rear Admiral A.K. Morehouse and sundry other lesser Aides. Rear Admiral Aubrey Dickenson RN, together with his Flag Lieutenant, Lt. Bowden, though outnumbered at this meting nevertheless represented a significant percentage of the naval forces available in the sector.

As well as the Royal Navy, Dickenson ruled over the on-station ships of the Royal Australian Navy, the Royal New Zealand Navy, the Royal Canadian Navy and maintained close cooperation with ships of the French and Royal Netherlands Navies represented.

A Columbian frigate operated in association with the US Navy and two frigates from Thailand also helped maintain a very warlike blockade of the Korean coasts. It had to be admitted however that what was lacking was a large enough and sufficiently capable army actually on the ground ashore. The General had a point.

"Gentlemen," the General began. " I have decided that a landing shall take place at Inchon. There are two reasons for this choice gentlemen; one is that that is the port from which the occupying US forces departed when power was handed over to the south Korean Government and the second is that

I'm damned if these damned commies are going to be allowed to think they can kick US arse.

"There is a major disadvantage to that particular port, from the point of view of landing an invading army and that is, I am informed by my Naval colleagues, that the rise and fall of tide in that port is thirty or more feet. That will make any beach landing either very long and therefore dangerous at low tide, or more or less impossible at high tide. I do not accept this interpretation.

"I believe that, for the reasons stated, we shall not be expected there and that this very difficulty will result in there being less resistance than we might otherwise expect. I have no desire to lose half my invading army staggering up some muddy beach under concentrated fire from dug-in shore batteries and trenches so gentlemen, we land at high tide. I don't care how you sailors do it but I want my soldiers put ashore with the least possible delay and in good order. Do I make myself clear?"

Admiral Joy looked at Rear Admiral Morehouse and they both looked at Rear Admiral Dickenson. Amongst the assembled Aides, an unrecognised voice was heard to mutter "shit!" The accent could have been either American or British, whichever it was, the sentiment was generally agreed.

"And, gentlemen, I do not want to be still standing here in three months time waiting for your proposals. I run the Military here and the military wants to be ashore by mid September! We have to relieve the pressure on the Pusan perimeter and I think that this is the way to do that"

Lieutenant Bowden followed his Admiral out of the office, retrieving his cap from amongst the many on the table by the door. "Not a lot of time, Sir. Less than six weeks!"

"It's not the time that worry's me Flags. It's the one thing he's forgotten."

"Forgotten?"

"Forgotten, or chosen not to remember. We have any number of aircraft carriers, they even have their battleship the mighty Mo; there are cruisers, destroyers, frigates, sloops, minesweepers and sundry other floating gun platforms. What we do not have Flags, is landing craft.

"When they'd pacified Japan, by 'forty six, the US navy decided that it would be impracticable to sail all their landing craft home to the good old US of A so they sold them off to the Japs for inter-island transports. Very grateful the Japs were too, I believe but it does leave us with a problem. How do we get the damned troops ashore?

"We certainly can't use troopships and just steam into Inchon harbour and tie up alongside like passenger liners as we did at Pusan, the north Korean army would regard that as just too cheeky.

"Methinks, young Bowden, we shall have to have a quiet word with our American cousins; someone has got to buy back all those boats."

"I don't think the present HM Government would authorise a contribution to such a purchase Sir, not without some copper bottomed guarantees that none of them would be sunk or damaged and that they would be guaranteed a return sale to their Japanese owners after their use in Korea. Of course, Sir, in theory, the UN should provide the landing craft if they want their army put ashore."

"You're learning Lieutenant. You're beginning to understand that the navy, at this level, has really very little to do with sailoring. Politics my boy, that's what makes the world go round. I think a meeting with Admiral Joy is required, sort it out will you."

* * *

"What do you mean, my relief hasn't been requested yet Scribes? I'm due home in a few months and I have a wife and child who want me back."

Able Seaman Arthurs stood at the half door of the ship's office, leaning on the little counter and looking at the Leading Writer who, accustomed to such problems, remained seated at his desk within.

"I've told you Arthurs, your relief can't be requested until three month prior and that ain't 'til next month. Now bugger off and let me get some work done."

"You will remind Jimmy about it though, won't you?"

"Yes, Bob, I will remind the First Lieutenant."

Challenger; the hands stood down from Action Stations to Defence Stations and then to Cruising Stations, had left the Formosa Strait and was now steaming at a sedate sixteen knots through the East China Sea, leaving the Ryukyu-retto to starboard.

In celebration of their easy victory over the Nationalist Chinese destroyer, if a victory it could really be called, the wardroom had invited the Captain to dinner. Leaving the junior officer, Sub Lieutenant Horton, the Gunnery Officer, as officer of the watch; they sat at table, comfortably full and glasses of port in hand.

"What next, do you think Sir? Will they let that merchant ship out again?"

"Oh I should think so Chas. No point in making trouble on their own doorstep. They will probably complain to the British government and the United Nations and no doubt to their American friends too but there's not a lot they can do now. They've lost."

"What about us, Sir?"

Commander Powers nodded to his Number One. "A good question Harry. What indeed? I intend taking my time getting back, to conserve fuel you understand but I have no doubt that sooner or later somebody will notice that we aren't wherever they want us to be and we shall receive the appropriate signal. You know how it is Harry, rush and wait, rush and wait. Well, for the moment, I intend to wait, quietly and enjoy our short cruise back to Japan."

The port was passed once more and glasses refilled. "What do you think will happen Sir? In Korea, I mean."

"Well, I imagine the army will have to outflank the North Koreans and land somewhere in the north of south Korea. Ideally, close enough to the border on the thirty eighth parallel to cut off military supplies and reinforcements reaching the south. Then, presumably, the South's army, aided and abetted by that of a reinforced United Nations, can sweep back up north and destroy the enemy or, at worst, chase them out of the country."

"Sounds as if we may be busy then, Sir. Lots more shore bombardments and stuff like that but it won't be much fun, eh?"

"Harry, we have both recently misspent five perfectly good years racing round the north Atlantic chasing submarines and shooting at impossible arial targets; I have no desire to repeat that experience. If my part in this war can be restricted to lounging about off-shore shooting at targets that can't shoot back, then I shall be well pleased. I have no desire to die young, nor even as a hero; my wife would never forgive me. Now, I must bid you good night. I have one or two things to do before I may turn in."

The officers all stood and wished him good night, then settled again on to the red leather upholstered seats around the switched-off electric fire in it's imitation grate while the stewards cleared the table behind them. Above them the fan turned slowly, doing little more than disturb the warm evening air.

"Well, I for one don't want to spend the next year or whatever driving up and down the coast of Korea, letting off a few fireworks from time to time. Whatever would I tell my grandchildren when I have them?"

"I doubt if we'll get the chance, Chas. The Ruskies are supplying the North Koreans and the Yanks are supplying the South Koreans. It's only a matter of time before the majors engage each other directly. Then the real fun will begin."

"What about the Russians also being on the Security Council of the United Nations though Number One? They can't fight each other directly without destroying the entire UN edifice."

"Welcome to the real world Chas! I reckon the UN will follow the League of Nations into the history books if that happens and then it will be every man for himself. Chaos."

"Not quite Number One, there is an alternative authority in NATO. All that will happen is that the Russians, Chinese and their allies will form a counter balancing organisation and there will be stalemate. Neither the Yanks nor the Ruskies will dare attack the other for fear of nuclear annihilation. No, I reckon that we'll see many years of minor, sniper-like attacks by an acolyte of one side against one from the other. Nothing too serious but I suspect that our long held hopes of peace and plenty are going to be denied. What we need is our own bomb or we'll end up doing whatever we're told by the Yanks and I don't fancy that."

Everyone present stared at the speaker, Engineer Lieutenant Darpin. "Well I never, plumber, that's very deep and I may say, deeply worrying don't you think?"

"I'm afraid it is and what's more, unless we get someone with real experience in government, we shall be caught with our knickers down again."

"You don't reckon our man Attlee then?"

"Middle class lawyer, more accustomed to handing out uplifting pamphlets and cheap meals in the east end of London than sorting out Stalin. I ask you, what sort of a competition would that be? We'd be on a hiding to nothing."

"Oh, I don't know plumber, he did serve as Churchill's deputy throughout the war."

"Precisely! That was to keep the unions on-side and that didn't always work!"

"Ah well, we've an election coming soon. You'd better get on your soapbox and do some serious converting. I suspect that most of the lads below will vote Labour again rather than risk going back to the pre-war ways."

"I'm not convinced of that Number One. I've never met a more conservative bunch than my lot. They may not be Tories but they sure as Hell ain't communists. I've heard 'em talking and, if I was a Labour candidate, I wouldn't reckon my chances in the stokers mess. As for the Chiefs and Petty Officers, I'd put them well to the right of Genghis Kahn"

"He's got a point Number One. I think most of the real sailors regard themselves as having been conned at the last election. A land fit for heroes and all that, no going back to the old ways, no more unemployment, free health care, free just about everything. They've worked out who has to pay for all this free largess."

"I think this discussion has gone far enough gentlemen. You know the rules of the mess. No politics, no sex and no religion. I suggest that we move on to some other, less disruptive subject. "

"But Number One, it makes no sense to ignore what is probably the most important decision that will have to be made; perhaps in their lifetime. If the Labour party is thrown out after just one short try at righting the wrongs of history, they may never get another chance."

"Enough Pilot. The subject is closed. I shall follow my learned Captain's example and retire, I think. Who knows what the morrow may bring."

"Probably a signal from FO2 FE, asking us why we aren't somewhere else."

"Very probably, Pilot. Good night gentlemen."

The short silence following the departure of the First Lieutenant was broken by Darling, unwilling to let the subject drop. "But it's important."

"You may well be right Pilot but the Jimmy's right too. The rules of the house are no politics, no sex and no religion even if that does restrict any really intelligent form of conversation. Anyone know anything about sport?"

The officers drifted off towards their respective cabins and the stewards tidied up behind them. Nothing much was going to change in the navy, whoever won the next election.

SEVEN

"Did you hear what that megalomaniac said?"

"What megalomaniac?"

"MacArthur!"

"Tell me."

"Apparently, and I have it on good authority Sir, he said that the landing at Inchon was a five Dollar bet to win fifty Dollars. Seems he's convinced that the surprise will more than make up for the difficulty of landing men on a defended coast with a thirty foot tide. I think he's mad, Sir."

"Well Flags, just as long as you don't tell me, you'll be alright."

They were back in their own office taking their evening drink; the Dakota flight back to Sasebo had been noisy and uncomfortable.

Admiral Dickenson shuffled through some papers and handed one of them to his Flag Lieutenant. "What do you think of that?"

Bowden read the paper he had been handed and handed it back. "Well, that makes a certain amount of sense, Sir. Who will you send?"

"Who have we got that isn't committed to something else?"

"Off hand, Sir, I'm not at all sure we have anyone that isn't already doing something else. I do wish these Generals wouldn't simply assume that the navy can spirit up a ship whenever they want one."

"I rather think Flags that that is what they fondly imagine the navy is for; a sort of transport service with guns.

"I imagine he wants some sort of bombardment first then lots of smoke and mirrors to convince them that this is the invasion and then, more smoke and mirrors whilst we get the poor bastards back by going alongside in the harbour they've just captured or, if it all goes wrong, off the beach."

"Powers said he was bored with west coast patrols, didn't he Sir? And, he's not actually committed at the moment, just en-route from the Formosa Strait; I'll set something up Sir. She's not due back until Tuesday."

Second Officer Archer poked her head through the open doorway, saw that they were still sitting there with their evening drinks and asked if there was anything she could do.

"No thank you Daphne. You can go home now. We'll close up."

"Thank you Sir but I have no desire to be sent home to the UK as redundant. I've got plenty to do to keep me occupied until you leave."

"Oh dear, I think I've hit a nerve."

"It's probably just that there has been a bit of talk about sending the girls home, out of harm's way, Sir."

"Not in this office there hasn't. And you may tell her that."

"I'm sure she'll be glad to hear it, Sir."

Daphne Archer knocked on the door again. "This has just been decoded Sir. Thought you would want to see it right away."

The admiral read the detailed report of Challenger's Formosa encounter with the Nationalist warship. Her previous signal had stated only that the City of Canterbury had entered harbour and that Challenger was returning to Japan.

"So, Powers hasn't started world war three; didn't think he would. Good man Powers but whatever you do, don't play poker with him. Now there's a happy coincidence."

"What's that, Sir?"

"Challenger. First thing tomorrow morning Flags, I want so see that Royal Marine Lieutenant, Owens."

"Oh yes, of course Sir. We have to organise the troops to go with her. Is that what you want to see Owens about?"

"No Flags. I have something altogether different in mind for him and for that matter, for Challenger before we worry too much about that. Have a word with MacArthur's man, get him to sort it out. It's his boss's idea; he can supply the troops. Meanwhile, tell Challenger to rendezvous about fifty miles west of Cheju-do. No need to tell them what for at this stage."

He walked out into the outer office smiling to himself; it might just be possible to get one up on MacArthur after all. That would be nice.

"Daphne, I think Lieutenant Bowden would appreciate your help with a few signals, if you don't mind. "

"Certainly Sir."

He smiled to himself as he closed the door behind him. Nice little girl and willing.

He wasn't supposed to know, of course that she had a crush, perhaps more than a crush, on Bowden.

General MacArthur looked at the report handed to him by his Chief of Staff. "Seems, the Chinese in Formosa have complained to Washington that the Brits are assisting the commies. Some Royal Navy ship helped a Limey merchant ship to enter one of the blockaded ports; threatened to sink the Chinese blockade ship if it interfered Sir."

"I thought they were supposed to be on our side? Have that Limey Admiral come and tell me about it. Tell him I'm not best pleased to have rude signals from Washington asking what the hell he's doing when I'm trying to win a real war here."

Almond nodded and knowing that his Aide had heard MacArthur, told him to ask Admiral Dickenson to call him.

"Never mind call you Edward! I want him here, on the mat. I won't have these damned Limeys doing their own thing while I'm in charge of this war. You just tell him that. I want an explanation and an assurance that he won't give any instructions that I haven't personally approved or I'll have him out of here! Is that clear?"

"It's clear enough Sir but I wouldn't recommend that my Aide puts it quite like that. As you say, Sir, we are supposed to be on the same side."

"He can put it how the Hell he likes but I want it clearly understood that I give the orders around here. This is my war; Truman put me in charge. You just make sure he knows that his job is to do as I tell him and not a single thing more!"

"I'm sure we'll think of a suitable form of words Sir. Now, this feint.

"We've asked Admiral Dickenson to organise the landing but we haven't detailed off the troops yet. I imagine you want the Marines to handle this?"

"Who else is there? If you want a job done properly, then you send for the US Marines."

"But, if we are asking the Brits to land them, it might be politic to invite them to provide some of their men too. Their Royal Marines are very good at this sort of thing. Plenty of experience."

"If you say so. Personally, I wouldn't use anyone but my own men if I could avoid it. I've trained 'em and brought them right the way across the Pacific, we've taken island after island and they're winners, every damned one of them. What do I know about these Royal Marines? Never had any serving under me before. OK, sort something out with them; just make good and damned sure that the American is in charge. I don't want some Limey deciding that he has a better idea and changing my orders."

Lieutenant Bowden read through the signals he had just drafted, made one or two grammatical corrections and kept the one for Challenger in his hand. "OK Daphne; that should do it for tonight. Fancy a drink before you go home?"

She hid her surprise. "Where Sir?"

"I thought we might go to the wardroom. Plenty of other people there, your reputation will be preserved. "

"Oh well, as long as my reputation is to be preserved, I suppose I can hardly refuse. I thought you were only allowed to take guests into the mess with prior permission of the President."

"Yes."

"So, this is a planned action. Am I to be allowed to know why you went to so much trouble when I might just as easily have declined your invitation."

"I hoped that you wouldn't. Anyway, you know most of the others and they know you."

"Will there be any other WRNS officers there tonight?"

"Actually, yes. First Officer Harbold is, as I imagine you know, engaged to Lieutenant Commander Edwards and he's invited her."

"You mean that only if I come can she and I am to be encouraged to come because she'll be there."

"It's not quite as cold blooded as that. I wanted you to come anyway. I want to buy you a drink."

"Oh well, if that's the only way poor Lieutenant Commander Edwards can get to take his fiancé in to the mess, I suppose I'd better come but I'm not dressed for dinner."

"We'll not be dining as a mess tonight. It's a free evening. I thought we might go on out somewhere after a drink and have dinner in town."

"So, it's all been worked out! I suppose I must act a chaperone for First Officer Harbold who, poor girl, is engaged to marry your friend Edwards but once her reputation has been protected by my attendance, we are, I take it, free to go on somewhere else and ruin my reputation privately?"

"Thank you."

"That's not the right answer. You're supposed to assure me that my reputation is as safe as the bank of England. Prior, that is, to the recent devaluation of the Pound."

"I meant, thank you saying you'd have a drink with me. I don't give a damn about Bunny Edwards' reputation nor that of the poor girl engaged to him. She could do worse, I imagine but it's none of my business. I think we had better get along there or this will get too complicated. We have to drop this signal for Challenger in to the wireless office on the way but that's all."

He held the door for her and closed it behind them. He took her arm. "I made a terrible mess of that, didn't I?"

"Yes but then, if you were clever, you wouldn't be the Admiral's doggy, would you?"

"Oh, I say, that's hardly fair. If I wasn't the Admiral's doggy, I wouldn't have met you and we wouldn't be having a drink together. Anyway, I'm not the Admiral's doggy, I'm his Flag Lieutenant; you've misunderstood the term."

"Then you'll have to explain it all to me."

"It'll be a pleasure. Now, I am the Admiral's Flag Lieutenant, that is, I'm the Admiral's right hand man without whom the entire Far East Fleet of the Royal Navy would come to a grinding halt. The Admiral's doggy is that entirely capable but far less dashing Able Seaman Browning. The term doggy indicates that the holder of that office fetches and carries for the Admiral, runs messages for the Admiral and generally acts as gofor."

"That's what I said Sir, you're the Admiral's doggy."

"I think you had better call me Terry if we are going for a drink and dinner and certainly if we're going to argue."

"I've never met a doggy called Terry before. Do you have a collar and lead?"

They walked in companionable silence to the wireless office and handed the signal to the Petty Officer Telegraphist of the watch. "One for Challenger Pots, OK?"

"No Problem Sir. I'll see to it."

"Thank you, goodnight."

The Petty Officer watched them walk away together noticing how close they were. Now there's interesting, he thought; he passed the signal to the duty Leading Tel. "Get that off hooky. Poor bastards aren't even going to get a run ashore it seems."

By the time they arrived at the wardroom door, an un-stated agreement had been arrived at. She was his girl and she was going to make good and sure that it stayed that way. She had had her eye on him ever since they had started working together and she was pretty sure that he had felt much the same about her. Why oh why are Englishmen so damned unsure of themselves? If he'd been a Yank, he would have chatted her up within minutes of deciding that she was attractive. Of course, if he had been a Yank, he would have been repulsed anyway but that's not the point. It had taken him almost six months to make his first move on her and she had, she had to admit, sometimes wondered if she had made a mistake in selecting him. God knew, there were hundreds of naval officers from seven or eight navies sculling about and she was an attractive woman. He should have got on with it months ago. ah well, everything comes to he or she who waits and there was no way he was going to escape now.

EIGHT

Lieutenant William 'Garry' Owens, an officer of 41 Independent Commando, Royal Marines, stood before the Admiral hoping that he was not here to be told that the mission was impossible. It was a good plan and he was the man to carry it out. Whilst the original idea had been the admiral's, admirals don't do things like this; Royal Marine Commandos do. True, a suitably qualified naval officer could have been selected but he knew that he was the best man available so he stood, at attention, in front of the admiral's desk, a half smile playing round his lips.

"Relax Owens. It seems that the major problem preventing us from carrying out our little plan has been resolved or at least, one part of it has. Our difficulty was in getting you on-site quickly and quietly; you will recall that we did not wish to involve the Americans." The young man nodded.

"In two days, a destroyer will be standing off Cheju-do. We can get you to the island on the mail flight but we still need to get you from the island to the ship. Any bright ideas?"

"Fast Patrol Boat Sir? The South Korean Marines have a base there. Failing that, I know a few people in the Yankee OSS who have a few people in the island, training the ROK people; I should be able to get a ride."

"If you say so Lieutenant, you've worked with them before, as you say. Get your kit and equipment sorted out and be on the mail flight tomorrow morning; I'll have my Flag Lieutenant lay it on. And, don't get yourself killed.

"You've been briefed by the clever buggers I take it?"

"Yes Sir. Thank you Sir, thanks a lot."

It was too good to be true, of course. Challenger's amble through the east China Sea towards Japan could not be allowed to continue. The jealous Gods, in the form of a signal from FO2, instructed them to proceed to a position 33.40N 126.30E and to notify their expected time of arrival.

"Doesn't sound like a routine west coast patrol Sir, I've asked Pilot to sort out our ETA but, as far as I can see, that position should put us about fifty miles west of the island of Cheju. I suppose it could be a rendezvous with an oiler, save us going back to Sasebo and the fleshpots"

"You're probably right Harry. No doubt our masters will make all clear in the fullness of time."

"That'd be a first, Sir!"

"Wouldn't it! Never mind, ours is not to reason why and all that."

The Navigating Officer appeared in the doorway of the Captain's cabin. "Got the figures here, Sir. If we continue at sixteen knots as we are, we should reach Cheju-do at 0600 the day after tomorrow, September first."

"Alright Pilot, draft a signal to that effect for FO2 and we'll see what happens. As the only thing we can alter is our speed, they may ask us to wind her up a bit but, sixteen knots is our economical cruising speed and our masters and his seem keen that we shouldn't burn any more fuel than is absolutely necessary. If FO2 wants us there sooner, he'll have to order us to increase speed. Damn silly way to fight a war but, since when was the Admiralty anything other than silly? No, that's not a question, don't answer that, there's no point in all three of us being tried for treason or whatever it is to question our masters."

"I think it's mutiny Sir but I won't tell them if you don't."

"Thank you Pilot, you've no idea what a great comfort

that is. Let me know when the signal's gone. What's our course?"

"Zero zero five degrees, Sir, all the way."

The Captain wound the handle on the direct line sound-power telephone in front of his desk. "Bridge? Alter course to 005."

"Zero zero five, Sir."

The officer of the watch repeated the order into the voice pipe in front of him. Even sitting in his chair, the Captain felt the ship heal slightly as the turn to port was made. "Course 005, Sir."

"Thank you." He replaced that telephone and lifted another from the row in front of him. "Plumber? What's our fuel state? It seems we aren't going back to Sasebo after all."

Engineer Lieutenant Darpin consulted the clipboard hanging on a hook in front of him. "Sixty five percent, Sir. What had you in mind?"

"Sorry Chief, I've no idea yet. We've been told to rendezvous off Cheju-do but not why. Of course, it could be an RV with one of the oilers but, at the moment, I have no idea. Better tell your people that we may be fuelling at sea at the crack of dawn on Tuesday, OK?"

"Very good, Sir. Should be no problem, providing the weather's fair to middling good."

"We'll be carrying on at ECS revs unless told otherwise so we shouldn't use too much on the way. We shouldn't have any problems even if it isn't a refuelling RV."

"That depends on whether you regard us as being half full or half empty when we reach fifty percent, Sir."

"As Captain, I regard fifty percent as being half full."

"As your Engineer Officer Sir, I shall regard that as being half empty and recommend refuelling as soon as practicable."

"Thank you Chief. Noted.

"Yes, Yeoman? What can I do for you?"

Yeoman Houseman stood behind the First Lieutenant in the doorway, a signal pad on the clipboard in his hand.

"The ETA has been sent, Sir and I thought you had better see this before the buzz gets round the ship. None of my lads would say a word, of course, but you know the navy, Sir." He handed the clipboard to the Captain.

"Have you seen this, Number One?"

"No Sir."

"Then you'd better. This is probably the hottest piece of news we've had since we started this war. This is going to go down very well with the people, I suspect."

He handed the signal to the First Lieutenant who read it through twice before handing it back to the Yeoman. " I know it only says 'Restricted' on the top of this signal but you are sworn to secrecy, Yeoman, is that understood?"

"Yes, I know, Sir, I signed the Act when I joined."

"Never mind the Official Secrets Act Yeoman, that's for shore-side. This is important and it will have to be announced properly by the Captain, not spread as a Tot-worthy rumour, OK?"

"Sir."

"Will you wait until after Sunday Prayers this morning Sir or accept that, by then, it will be all round the ship. You could Tannoy throughout the ship Sir. Might ensure that they get the figures right and that there are no nasty surprises later although I see that the precise definition of War Zone is to follow."

"Good idea Harry. Ask the duty electrician to sort it out, will you. I'll broadcast it from here as soon as it's laid on. I don't think we need to worry too much about their definition of war zone, it must include where we've been."

"If you say so, Sir. I hope you're right."

Harry Enders had the duty electrician piped to report to his cabin and went there to wait for him to appear.

"Good news, ain't it Sir."

"What?"

"About the Gratuity sir."

The first Lieutenant hid his smile that the news was already round the ship. The navy had ways of spreading rumours only surpassed, he suspected, by the church.

"You have not heard that rumour sparks. Do I make myself clear?"

"Oh absolutely, Sir. Certainly I didn't get it confirmed by the First Lieutenant Sir."

"Before I have you charged with something very nasty sparks, the Captain wants you to set up his cabin microphone for a broadcast throughout the ship. I've no idea what he wants to tell them but, if I were you, I'd get it sorted as quickly as you can.; your next promotion might just depend upon it."

"Oh you wouldn't Sir!"

"Oh yes I would."

"D'y'hear there. This is the First Lieutenant speaking. The Captain has an announcement to make that concerns every one of us and I want you to listen very carefully to what he has to say."

"This is the Captain speaking. I have just been notified that, as from the commencement of hostilities in this theatre, all ranks shall be entitled to payment of a War Zone Gratuity. As I understand it, this gratuity shall amount to ten Pounds for the first twenty eight days consecutive service in the Korean War Zone and one Pound per month thereafter. Not what you might call generous but it is something entirely new and I am happy to be able to tell you about it.

"I imagine the Admiralty will advise me when to pay this gratuity, it goes without saying that it won't be a cash bonus but added to your normal pay. I'm sure that the Paymaster in Sasebo will be at this very minute, poised over his abacus or whatever he uses to calculate our pay so that there will be no unreasonable delay in its disbursement.

"The First Lieutenant has, very wisely I think, advised me that the signal we have received does not actually define this Korean War Zone but I have no reason to doubt that we shall all be at least ten Pounds better off very shortly, perhaps a little more as we've already been here some time. That is all."

Even in the rarefied atmosphere of the Captain's Day Cabin, the cheering throughout the ship could be heard clearly but then, Challenger was a small ship and the Captain's cabin was separated from the rest of the ship by a matter of only a few yards and two vertical ladders.

"Well, that should make 'em happy, Sir."

"One more joke like that Harry and you'll find yourself in Aisne."

"God, that's worse than mine!"

"Imagine how it feels for those poor souls who are in her. Can't you just imagine. Some fool asks you what ship you're in and you have to reply I'm in Aisne."

"That sounds like bitter experience Sir."

"It is Number One. I was in her forty seven and forty eight."

"Oh, hard luck Sir. You won't mind if I tell the others, will you? It might get you the sympathy vote."

"I wasn't aware that I needed it."

"Who can foretell the future, Sir?"

They heard the ship's Tannoy PA system turned on again. "Hands to Divisions on the upper deck."

"Come on Number One. We have duties to perform. Where the Hell did I put that bible?" He picked up the book and his hat. "Get 'em fallen in Number One. I'll be up in a minute."

On the upper deck, the hands fell in by their Divisions, each fronted by their Chief or Petty Officer who checked that all were present. These reported to the Divisional Officer who in turn, reported to the First Lieutenant.

It was hot, even dressed in their number six uniforms of white cotton but not uncomfortable.

"Looks good Number One."

The Captain looked at the ship's company, drawn up on the fo'c'sle. "As they have just been given a pay rise, I think I'll inspect the lot today! Then they can listen to me offering up a prayer not only for their preservation from the forces of evil but mine also; something about which I care very strongly. I'll even pray for those that aren't here, those that are on watch. That should give them something to worry about."

"Do you think that's entirely fair, Sir"

"No but if I don't know where we're going or what for and I'm pretty sure they don't either so I don't think a short prayer will do any harm. I might even thank God for the ten pounds whilst I'm about it."

"Not bad, eh Hooky? Ten quid for risking our health in the Japanese brothels and another Pound a month if we keep it up."

"You couldn't keep it up for long enough to satisfy a real woman, Martin. They all fake it you know, these pros."

"I don't care. So long as I gets my oats, that's their problem."

" If you ever get married mate, your wife will expect you to give her pleasure. She'll want to believe that you get pleasure from making her feel good, satisfied. Your satisfaction is easy, a quick hand flip and you're satisfied."

"Bugger all that mate, in this world, its every man for himself; that's what I say."

"Well don't say it to your wife if you ever get one. That'll turn her off for sure and once off, you'll have a Hell of a job turning her on again."

"And there speaks the voice of experience, eh Hooky?"

"Take my word for it mate. Be told."

"Still the ten quid ain't bad, eh?"

"But whose ten quid is it? Tell me that."

"I don't know. Taxes I suppose."

"And, who pays those taxes? You do you silly bugger. It's your own ten quid they're giving you. Big deal!"

"Well, its ten quid I wouldn't have got if they weren't, ain't it."

"You're thick Signalman Martin. There has to be a catch in it somewhere, there always is and you can bet your arse you'll end up paying for it yourself."

"Not with my arse, I won't so that's alright, eh?"

For the last twenty four hours, it had been almost the sole topic of discussion throughout the ship. Every messdeck had it's own opinion and every messdeck's lawer had given his; almost universally against.

Not against accepting the ten quid. That, happily, wasn't an option; that would have presented them with a terrible conflict of interest – throw out their principles and take the money or keep their self esteem and refuse the ten quid.

Fortunately, they had no choice. The ten pounds would be added automatically to their pay; they couldn't be blamed for that. Here, in the watch keeper's mess, the subject had been examined from all aspects; far more thoroughly than the distant Government could have imagined. Politicians, coming almost entirely from the educated middle class, assumed quite naturally that the common soldiery, which included sailors and airmen, would doff their caps, take the money and be grateful; but things were different now.

A major social change had been brought about during the second World War – not by the initial defeats nor by the later victories but by the, albeit friendly, occupation of large sections of England by young and independently minded Americans.

The labour party had been quick to recognise the advantage that this gave them in fighting the first post-war general election. No return to the bad old Tory days and ways, they had offered. A new Britain, a Socialist Britain, a Britain governed by the people for the people; Christ, they'd almost gone as far as claiming that they were in favour of the people's entitlement to the pursuit of happiness.

It had been the service vote that had swung it. The soon to be demobilised common soldiery that had had enough of yes Sir, no Sir, three bags full Sir. They wanted and had voted for a more democratic Britain, a Britain in which the ordinary man made the rules and for that reason, everyone would keep to them.

How long had it taken for them to realise that, if anything, things were worse? The new, Labour government had retained the wartime government's draconian powers for the direction of labour, had actually reduced some food rations and had even rationed things that had not been rationed during the darkest days of the war.

Houses, requisitioned by local Authorities during the war had not been handed back to their owners but been kept and everyone knew that their allocation to tenants by the Council's Housing Department was dictated by bribery, political affiliation or, in some cases, in return for sexual favours.

How much of this was true didn't matter, it was generally believed; particularly amongst the still serving servicemen. Far from home they were unable to take any practical part in directing the creation of the new Britain they had been promised. And now there was another war and all the same mistakes were being made again.

This time however, the man at the front knew the score; they had seen it all before. The second World War had been too recent, most of the men now serving had taken part in it. Slogans wouldn't work this time. Cynicism had already kicked in, letters from home reported that walls had already been daubed with sardonic slogans such as 'Make the army you're

Korea' and, more importantly, 'NO! Let the politicians fight this time.'

It hadn't taken long for the socialists to fall out amongst themselves. In Europe, Russia, good old Uncle Joe, was now the enemy; that had taken all of about three years and now here, in Asia, the communist North Koreans were fighting the nominally capitalist south Koreans and socialist Britain was on the side of the capitalists! And they expected the public to believe a word they said? Just let them wait!

NINE

To the west, the sun dipped momentarily below the horizon then flared up again for just a second, as if reluctant to leave the stage to the moon which was already visible to the east. Lying on its back, already exhausted by a hard day's work on the other side of the world, the moon ignored the gesture, secure in the knowledge that the night was hers.

"They'll have to tell us where we're going soon, Sir."

Lieutenant Chas Turner was officer of the watch and the Captain had come up on to the bridge to take the already cooler air; until his arrival, Chas Turner had been sitting comfortably in the Captain's sea chair but had relinquished it immediately.

"I imagine so Chas. All in God's good time, eh?"

"But we usually know, don't we Sir."

"Well, at 0600 tomorrow morning, we should be in our RV position and something should happen. Unless, of course, the signal was a forgery sent by the enemy who have left a mine in that position for us to run on to. I suppose that's possible."

"Then they must have more faith in Pilot's navigation than I do, Sir. There's a hell of a lot of sea out there and such pin-point accuracy is impossible."

"Oh ye of little faith Chas. I'm sure young Darling's navigation is of the best. I'd have had him out of here long ago if it hadn't been."

"He is a bit left wing though, Sir. You don't think its all some big communist plot to sink Challenger?"

"I doubt it. And, he'll grow out of that anyway."

"Well, I hope he does that before he gets us sunk."

"Nice evening, eh Sir?" The First Lieutenant stepped up on to the raised wooden gratings of the bridge from the ladder at the back of the bridge. Below the gratings a tracery of steam pipes, had not been used since the ship's arctic convoy duties six years before. "It occurred to me Sir. If this war isn't over in a couple of months, and they send us up to the north of the Yellow sea to do bombardments in winter, we might need to make certain the steam pipes are working."

"That's what I like to see Number One. Forethought. If this war isn't over by the winter, it isn't going to be over for some time and a whole new set of rules will have to be thought out."

"Like, whose going to pay for it, eh Sir? Us or the United Nations and, if it's the UN, how are they going to raise the wind?"

"I suspect that they will ask us for the money Chas; us and all the other members, of course. If they do that, it will be interesting to see how many still want to be members badly enough to actually pay for it. It's a good club to be in if you're a small country of course, it lets you shout the odds against much bigger, stronger countries who have the same single vote as you do but it will be interesting to watch and that's all that you and I shall be able to do ; we are in the hands of the politicians."

"Then, God help us."

" Well, look at it this way Chas. When was the last general election?"

"Nineteen forty five, Sir."

"And what year is this?"

"Nineteen fifty Sir; oh, I see. You mean that there must be an election this year or early next."

"Correct. And, if this war isn't over by then, it will be an interesting event. Will the country vote for another war so soon after the last one? What do you think Number One?"

"I think that this is a very dangerous subject Sir and one banned in the Mess. I don't think I want to discuss it at all."

"Very sensible Harry. I agree, it was an unfair question. I have no business asking you such a question when your future promotion depends upon my recommendation and that could, at least in theory, be influenced by any answer you might give to such a question. I withdraw it absolutely. Your promotion is safe, providing you don't deflower my daughter."

"You haven't got a daughter Sir, have you?"

"The threat was hypothetical, Harry."

Below, his steward had laid the table for dinner and was chafing at the bit to get it done and to get back to the book he was reading, The Nightlife of the Gods by Thorne Smith; funniest book he'd ever read.

Thorne Smith, the frequently less than sober son of a US Navy Commodore had given up sailoring himself and had established a reputation for writing some of the funniest books in print.

* * *

"Captain Sir." The officer of the watch leaned over the voice pipe to the Captain's sleeping cabin immediately below the bridge. "O Five three O, Sir. You asked for a call."

"Thank you Number One. Anything in sight?"

"Not a thing Sir. No signals received and nothing visible on radar. If I hadn't checked Pilot's calculations, I could believe that we were in the wrong place."

"We have half an hour yet Harry. Like Mr Macawber, we'll just have to hope that something turns up."

"I admire your sangfroid Sir. I don't like surprises."

"Organise some coffee Harry, I'll be up in a minute."

The bridge messenger nodded in understanding of the order and disappeared down the ladder towards the wardroom pantry and, he hoped, coffee. If the wardroom stewards had none made yet, he would have to go on down to the wardroom galley; they would be up and about by now. The hands had been called at five o-clock and the ship was well alive below decks.

The Captain's head appeared above the hatch at the back of the bridge.

"Still nothing Number One?"

"No Sir. Quiet as the grave."

"Very well. Hands to defence stations, just in case, eh?"

The pipe was made and the ship moved from Cruising stations to Defence stations, one step down from Action stations.

All over the ship, men moved into their Defence Stations positions, Additional lookouts closed up, guns crews loitered close to their guns, ready to jump to it if the klaxon was sounded. Ready use ammunition lockers were opened and ammunition checked. If the Old Man pressed the klaxon alarm for Action Stations, everything would be ready.

"Bridge, Plot. We have an aircraft bearing green one five, ten miles, approaching."

"Just the one Pilot?"

"Just the one, Sir. Something odd about it though Sir, doesn't seem to be going fast enough."

"Keep an eye on it Pilot. Action Stations please Number One. Just in case."

The reports came in immediately. "Action Stations closed up, Sir."

"Thank you Number One. That has to be the fastest ever, they must be enthusiastic this morning. Director, have you the aircraft bearing green one five?"

"Yes Sir, on him now. Main armament, follow Director. Secondary armament aircraft bearing green one five, eight miles. Main armament high explosive, load, load, load."

Below the bridge, the gun's crews of 'A' and 'B' guns drew the first shells from the ready use locker, the number three man passing the shell to the loader and the number four man passing the cordite cartridge to the second loader. The officers on the bridge could hear the breach slam shut as the gun barrel traversed from fore and aft to green one five, following the gunnery director above and behind the bridge.

The Gunnery Officer had the best , albeit electronic, view and could control all the main armament at the same time. All four guns reported that they were loaded with HE.

"Bridge, Director. All guns loaded HE. Following Director. Director locked on target."

"Thank you Guns. Let's hope we don't need you, eh?"

"It's a fine morning for it, Sir. Clear as a bell. You have him visual already. Doesn't seem to be interested in taking avoiding action or anything like that Sir. Almost as if he hasn't seen us."

"Sillier things have happened Guns. Keep your eye on him."

A shout up the voice pipe from the wireless office below made the Yeoman bend his ear to it. "Yeo? Have a Yankee helicopter on Voice, says he has a passenger for us. You want me to put it through up there?"

"Yes. Captain Sir. Wireless Office reports that they have a Yankee helicopter on Voice channel. Says they have a passenger for us."

"Thank you Yeoman. Is it put through to you up here now?"

"Yes, Sir."

"Let me have the mic will you."

"American helicopter, this is Challenger. If you're the target all my guns are locked on to, you'd better identify yourself a bit sharpish, over."

"Hell, Man. What d'y'want? My phone number?"

"I want to be sure that the chopper I can see is the one I'm talking to. Guns, one round, not to close please."

"'B' gun, only, one round for effect, deflection starboard two degrees. Shoot."

The watchers saw the brown puff of the explosion just to starboard of the helicopter.

"Shit Man! You don't play games, do you? I am descending to sea level then rising immediately to the original height, course and speed; that do you?"

"That will do for starters. What do you want?"

"I have a passenger for you. My instructions were to find you and deliver Lieutenant Owens to you. He's one of yours."

The watchers saw the chopper perform the manoeuvre described.

"Helicopter, this is Challenger I will lower a boat. You may drop your passenger as close to it as possible. I take it he can swim?"

"Guy says yes."

"Number One. Away sea boat's crew. Tell them to stand off about a hundred yards or so and wait for some idiot to jump out of the helicopter then pick him up and bring him back to me."

"Aye aye, Sir.

The seaboat, the twenty seven foot whaler, was lowered on its falls and at the right moment, the disengaging gear dropped it into the sea.

"Seaboat away, Sir."

"Thank you Number One. Now we wait Helicopter, this is Challenger, you may deliver your passenger then fly on reciprocal course for ten miles. Any deviation may result in your destruction. Is that understood?"

"Your order received and understood Sir I'm glad you're on our side."

"I'm not, young man. I'm on my side and I don't take chances."

The chopper hovered, dropping lower and lower over the seaboat, drenching the crew by stirring up the water around them. At the last possible moment, it side-slipped and a man was seen jumping from the Perspex bubble into the water.

The aircraft rose, instantly, turning on to the course ordered and cranking up to full speed as quickly as possible. "Thank you helicopter and goodbye. I recommend that the next time you have to do this job, you organise some form of recognition signal before you arrive. It will be altogether safer."

"You can say that again, Buddy. If you're friendly, I'd sure as hell hate to meet any of the other British ships."

"Lieutenant Owens, Royal Marine Commandos, Sir. Sorry about all that but it was important that there was no chance of a security leak or signal intercept and there wasn't time for you to pick me up from Sasebo."

"Ah, Hello Royal. Well, at least you're dry. I was worried about that. What's this all about?"

The Marine handed Powers the sealed envelope he was clutching in his right hand. "Could we discuss it in your cabin Sir?"

"If you insist. Stand down Action Stations Number One. Leave the Plot at Defence Stations and stand down the rest. If this is all as secret as it appears, I want to know if we are being shadowed by another aircraft or even a submarine; theirs or ours!"

"Very good, Sir."

The captain pointed to a spare chair in his cabin. "Sit, whilst I read this": he indicated the envelope which he was opening with a particularly vicious looking knife. Noticing the marine's interest in the weapon, he smiled. "Took it off a very drunken Able Seaman years ago; I was Officer of the Day on a converted trawler; he said it was for gutting fish."

A few minutes silence passed until he placed the orders on his desk.

"We should be able to manage. A bit 'Boy's Own Paper', eh?"

"Rather, Sir."

"You'd better bunk in with my First, Harry Enders; do you know him? I take it you have all the kit you want?"

"Don't think I know Enders but I'm sure we'll be get along fine, it's only a few days anyway. I've got everything I shall need Sir. If I can't carry it on my back, I can't have it. Simple really."

"But uncomfortable I suspect but that's your problem; let me know if you do need anything OK? I take it everything I'm allowed to know is in these orders you've just given me?"

"I hope so, Sir."

The Captain's steward appeared in answer to the bell. "This is Lieutenant Owens, Masters. He'll be bunking in with the First Lieutenant.   See to it, will you."

"Sir."

The telephone on the bridge rang twice before being answered.

"Number One. I'm afraid I've invited our guest to bunk in with you for a few days. Best if he's not asked too many questions."

"Very Good, Sir. I'll deal with it."

*   *   *

The wardroom was crowded. All officers not actually needed anywhere else had been assembled for this meeting. The Captain stood up and, in doing so, obtained their undivided attention; nobody wanted to miss this, this was going clearly going to be something special.

"Now, Gentlemen. This meeting is to introduce you all to Lieutenant Garry Owens, Royal Marines. He is coming with us up north or, more accurately, we are taking him up north.

"As I understand it, the plan is for us to sneak in as close as we can safely to Inchon and to land Lieutenant Owens on one of the islands in the Flying Fish Channel.

"You are all aware of course, being good naval officers, that there are a lot of small islands adjoining and within the channel which is the only main channel into that port. We have to assume that these islands are now occupied by enemy forces with aggressive capability and whilst I don't know just what Lieutenant Owens proposes doing about it, I'm sure he will think of something.

"Initially, at least, he will be locating, identifying and reporting the positions of any seaward facing guns and, somehow, he intends to move from island to island without being either caught or killed. I wish him luck! Pilot. Your job is to get him in and then get us out again without attracting too much attention; arrange times and all that with Owens and let me know. Clear?"

"Absolutely Sir."

"Good. There is nothing for the rest of you to do but be nice to him, this is probably his last week on earth."

For a moment, silence reigned then a hubbub of question and answer broke out. Everyone wanted to shake hands with Owens and everyone wanted to know exactly what he was intending to do and how he was intending to do it.

The discussion was as open as it could be, given that Owens himself was unsure just what he did intend to do but as there was no chance of careless talk tipping off the enemy, such answers as he did give were honest and enough to cause a mixture of alarm and admiration. Nobody in their right mind would attempt to do what Lieutenant Owens intended.

The joy of a detached command has been recognised by

those commanders fortunate enough to be granted this freedom from supervision by senior officers since King Alfred assembled the first English fleet – and probably in other, earlier navies, since man first travelled upon the sea.

To be so fortunate as to be selected as he had for two such detachments, back to back as it were, singled out Commander David Powers in Challenger as the most fortunate of naval officers. However, as any naval officer will confirm, such freedom from supervision carries with it the burden of total responsibility for not only his ship but also for the success of the project upon which it is engaged.

Lunch was over and the ship's routine re-established. On the bridge, the officer of the watch and the signalman leant in an almost leisurely manner against the forebridge canopy. The sky was clear and blue and the warmth of the afternoon sun gave an almost holiday atmosphere to the men on watch.

That they were relaxed did not mean that they were inattentive. The lookouts swung their binoculars through the arc between right ahead and right astern, looking for aircraft that the radar should have spotted already. The officer of the watch was desperately trying to remember the words of a current comedy song, something to do with a fox raiding a chicken run. He asked the signalman if he could remember them.

Signalman Sallis looked pained that an officer should have such an infantile choice of favourite song but provided the answer.

"There ain't nobody here but us chickens
there ain't nobody here at all
so hush yo mouth, don't make no fuss
there ain't nobody here but us. Sir."
"Ah yes. Clever isn't it?"
"If you like that kind of thing, Sir."

TEN

The dogs stood outside the cookhouse, waiting either to be fed from scraps or to be chased away depending upon which Sergeant Cook was on duty this morning. There were now six of them. There had originally been three then five and by tomorrow, there would be at least seven; the word or was it the woof, had gone round.

Here, in the base camp rapidly established by X Corps and made up from the First Division of the US Marines and the Seventh Infantry Division, they were safe from anything more than being chased away from the food they desperately needed. Anywhere else in Korea, they would have been in danger of being the food that the refugees from the war so desperately needed.

They were in luck. Sergeant Thomas was a softy, a Marine Corps softy but a softy just the same when it came to dogs. At home his father bred Airdale Terriers, a rare breed in the States and sired by the descendents from a pregnant bitch secreted amongst his father's kit when he had been shipped home from England when the war ended. She had repaid his father's generosity and love by presenting him with a litter of seven beautiful pups, every one perfect.

At the family farm, these had grown big and strong and, by means of the American Kennel Club newssheet, found others of their breed with which to be mated. His father now made more money from breeding the dogs than he did from the farm from which he had anyway now retired. Sergeant Thomas's younger brother now ran the farm and Sergeant Thomas ran the best cookhouse in the US Marine Corps and he was happy with this arrangement.

He supervised the serving of the last of the breakfasts to the hungry soldiers and insured that the washing up was in hand before gathering up the scraps scraped from the plates, not much from a bunch of hungry soldiers and marines but enough to guarantee the dogs at least one more day. Who knew? In a few days, the soldiers may well be gone and the dogs once more reduced to scavenging amongst the locals who were probably not as well fed as they had been for the last few days.

Sergeant Thomas knew dogs so he didn't waste his time wondering where they had come from. Dogs, hungry dogs, could smell food from miles away and the meat-rich food served to the US military would have been detectable from even further. Tomorrow there would be more dogs and, the day after that, even more; there would be no end to it until the Medics decided that they represented a health hazard and the military police would do a sweep through the camp and catch as many as they could. These would be driven many miles away and turned loose to inevitably find their way back to the camp whilst those which had avoided the swoop would be outside the cookhouse again the following morning waiting, expectantly for whatever a benevolent God would dispense.

The marines and the infantry soldiers in camp Xray had been withdrawn from the Pusan perimeter, relieved by fresh troops brought in from Japan and spirited secretly to this new camp from which there was to be no leave, no passes to the local village and its bars. There wasn't a local village. They had seen no other human habitation anywhere near the tented camp that the first contingent had themselves erected. Camp Xray was uncomfortable, unknown to the Post Office and there was no serious danger of the PX finding it and setting up a branch.

Rumour had it that this camp had been set up on the personal instruction of Major General Almond, MacArthur's chief of staff himself and if that were true, there had to be a reason for it; from the look of the place and the speed with which it had been erected, there was very little chance of that reason becoming known until Almond was good and ready to tell them.

They were now well behind the front line, they couldn't even hear the artillery from here, not even at dead of night. If they had been withdrawn this far from the fighting, there had to be a very good reason for it.

Day by day, more units of the First Division of the US Marine corps arrived, shipped direct, initially from Japan and subsequently from all over the world; no one knew what for but everyone knew now that, whatever it was it was going to be something big. A new Commanding Officer had been appointed, a veteran of the Pacific War and a much respected fighting man and that could only mean that there was some serious fighting to be done and that they were going to be doing it. Sergeant Thomas didn't much care. He was a professional, he had been a Marine since '43 and he would go where he was sent; meanwhile, he would feed the dogs; giving them life made him feel better about all the killing that would have to be done.

He hadn't mentioned it to anyone and no one had mentioned it to him but the latest delivery of equipment had come by sea and had been delivered by the kind of landing craft he remembered all too clearly from their island hopping progress across the Pacific. Something told him that whatever it was they were going to do, it probably involved those landing craft; otherwise why hadn't they backed off from the beach and gone back to wherever they had come from. He hated these LST's, big, ungainly, tank carrying beasts of boats with flat bottoms and an ability to roll on wet grass. Sergeant Thomas was no fool; those LST's meant a beach landing somewhere and experience told him that that almost certainly meant somewhere behind the enemy's front line.

* * *

As a guest, Lieutenant Owens was placed on the right of the First Lieutenant at dinner. From the other end of the table, Sub Lieutenant Horton caught his eye, during a lull in the general conversation. "Have you heard about this ten quid our Lords and Masters are going to pay us for getting shot at?"

"I've heard about it of course but nobody's given me any money yet."

"If your little junket is just half as dangerous as I think it is Royal, you'll never get it."

Owens saw the purple coloured felt between the two rings on the new speaker's jacket and recognised it as the engineering branch "Its probably not as dangerous as it sounds, Chief. These things never are. All I've got to do is swim ashore from your boat, its too risky taking the boat right in, and wander about noting the positions of the enemy's guns. As most of their soldiers will be close to those guns and the islands are otherwise uninhabited, all I have to do is keep a low profile and keep quiet; doddle, actually. I think I'm probably safe enough as long as you or your friends don't start bombarding the island while I'm actually on it."

"How do you propose getting the information back to whoever wants it, Royal?"

"I've got a lovely new toy, a small transceiver. I transmit on a fixed frequency at any time and my signal is recorded automatically back at base. That means that they don't have to have someone manning that frequency all the time, they leave it on speaker and play back the recording. Marvellous, ain't it? It also means that there's no regular pattern of transmissions for the enemy to lock on to."

"What happens if they want to talk to you?"

"I listen in at a fixed time each day. If the enemy hear it, their direction finder will simply show that the transmitter is in Sasebo or somewhere down there. No danger to me."

"Well, good luck. How do you get back to what passes for civilisation?"

"Oh, I imagine someone will come and get me eventually."

"It will probably be us that comes back for you. We're due for another patrol up and down this coast. All we'd have to do is slow down to swimming speed and you could clamber back on board. If you ask him nicely, Number One will leave a ladder down each time we pass."

"You all seem to take it very casually. Have you done many of these patrols?"

"Too many but we get a bit of excitement from time to time. You know, we go close in and bombard something, usually a train or a convoy of lorries on the coast road and just occasionally, they're kind enough to send out a few small boats or send a couple of aircraft over so young Guns here can practice his anti-aircraft gunnery."

"Oh, I say Chief, that's hardly fair. I haven't put you down."

"But you're the youngest, Sub. Its traditional."

Owens took pity on the youngster. "The way I heard it Sub, the Yanks have lost a couple of ships to air attack or mines. I heard that one of the two Siamese boats was lost too. It can't be quite as easy as you suggest."

"But they're foreigners, Royal. They don't count. By the way, I think we're supposed to call them Thai now, not Siamese."

"If you say so. I must have an old atlas."

The last of the night's moon passed behind a bank of cloud and Challenger glided almost silently in towards Inchon and the entrance of the Flying Fish Channel.

"I daren't go much closer in Royal. They're bound to have some kind of radar on the biggest island, Wolmi. We know that that's heavily fortified so they must have some form of direction system for their guns and that presumably includes radar."

"We'll drop the seaboat here and get you in closer. You say you don't want the boat to actually drop you on the beach?"

"Daren't Sir. When the tide goes out there might be marks on the mud showing where we had landed, better if I get a little wet and dirty than that we give the game away right at the beginning."

"OK Royal, if that's the way you want it. Tell the Coxswain when you think you're close enough. I take it you'll have dry clothes and your radio and all that in the waterproof bag you brought with you; the one you dropped from the helicopter before you jumped yourself."

"Just the radio and a few other things that matter. Dirty clothes will help me merge into the background better."

"Suit yourself. OK Number One, stop the ship and drop the seaboat. Tell the coxswain we'll be back for him in two hours. He's to get as far from the land as possible by then and wait for us to spot him. No lights or flares or anything silly like that, eh? We'll find him using the short range radar. Tell him, if we can't find him, he's to row back to Sasebo and we'll follow."

"If I told him that, Sir, he'd probably be back there before we get back to here."

Beneath the badinage, they all knew that the young lieutenant was going to have a very uncomfortable and almost certainly very dangerous few days ashore. No one would mention it.

ELEVEN

Camp Xray was busy, busier than it had been since its establishment, and that's saying something. Three more big LST's had arrived. Tents now extended as far as the eye could see and equipment could be seen everywhere; some static in carefully labelled batches, ready for reloading on to the LST's and more being organised into batches ready for loading.

Everywhere men hurried, chased by Sergeants who were in turn being chased by Lieutenants. The army never changes, rush and wait, rush and wait; somewhere, someone might know what was going on but the soldiers on the ground seldom did. When they were told what was expected of them, it was always too late to suggest an alternative; even if anyone would have been prepared to listen to it.

The latest LST's to arrive had carried tanks and bulldozers and these had been driven ashore and were being put through a routine of testing to make sure that, when they next went ashore, wherever that might be, they would work

Their big engines roared as their drivers gunned them up to maximum revs and let them fall off again, to see if they would stall. Those that did would be taken away and played with by the motor engineers until they performed like Swiss watches; there was no room for error in a landing. If just one of those beasts stalled or failed to start on time, it could block the entire shipload of other tanks and the vital stores behind them. Sitting on the beach with its big doors open, an LST was an easy target for the shore side gunners.

Stores were being checked and allocated to ships. The petrol, diesel fuel and ammunition required by the tanks and trucks and the guns to follow them ashore must be on the right ship, in the right quantity and in easy to man-handle loads. There must be no mistakes when the bow doors opened; when the Landing Officer said Go, Go it must.

The new Commanding Officer had set up his head quarters and his Staff was busy developing the details of the plan laid down in general terms by the Supreme Commander MacArthur, to the accompaniment of the usual grumbles. It was alright for him, sitting there in Tokyo but for the Marines and the Infantrymen who were expected to get ashore, knock out any immediate defence installations and establish the beachhead, it wasn't that simple. For them, there would be resistance, real resistance; fighting men like themselves, fighting men who would fight.

The point of all this planning was to limit, as far as humanly possible, the number of casualties Force X would suffer. If they got it wrong, if it was based on inaccurate intelligence or some idiot made a simple mistake in a calculation somewhere, disaster threatened. Everything was checked and checked again by someone else to make sure that the operation would be as successful as it was possible to make it. Intelligence was the thing, there was never enough of it.

Many of these officers, would be going ashore with the men and they had no desire to be listed as missing or dead; they too had families at home and would leave the heroics to the film stars safely back home in Hollywood. This was for real and you could very easily get very dead, very quickly if you were even ever so slightly unlucky.

The dog sweep-up feared by the cook had taken place on the second morning after the arrival of the new commanding officer. Obviously some Staff officer had spotted the dogs and decided that a few brownie points could be accumulated by first advising the new CO of the dog's existence and then that he had arranged for them to be swept up and got rid of. In any army, brownie points were to be attracted whenever possible. There were hundreds, possibly thousands of junior lieutenants and if they wanted to get to be generals, they need as many brownie points as possible. Get yourself noticed, that was the secret of success and promotion, nobody would remember later why you had been noticed by your CO and favoured, only that you got to be a captain that much sooner than the others.

* * *

Far to the north of all this activity, Lieutenant Owens lay on the short, scrubby grass observing the island in front of him. He had laid there for nearly half an hour now and his eyes were accustomed to the darkness and his nose to the smell of the vegetation around him and the mud on the beach behind him. He hadn't moved since landing and he wouldn't do so until he was satisfied that his arrival had not been seen by a sentry who was, even now, waiting somewhere out of sight for him to move, to expose himself in silhouette against the night sky behind him.

There were no trees here, just a few scrub bushes that had somehow become established on what was little more than a slightly raised mud bank deposited by the slowly flowing river that had formed the channel. In places it had gauged out the channel whilst, at others, it had deposited the silt it had released into little piles that, in time, had become these small islands.

Seeds, dropped or excreted by land-based birds had brought life to the exposed and drying mud and fishermen had learned that the sea birds gathered above the shoals of small fish in the channels and around the islands and had driven posts into the mud in the shallows from which to suspend their nets.

Lieutenant Owen was satisfied. Nothing had moved in the half hour he had been watching. He had not smelled another human being, lying as still as himself; he was satisfied that he was alone, that his arrival had not been seen by the enemy. He had learned a valuable lesson in Malaya when hunting for terrorists in the jungle; the smell of toothpaste or soap on his body or of cigarette smoke on his uniform could be smelled from quite a distance by a nose that had become accustomed to the natural smells of the jungle. He hadn't washed for two days and, happily, he didn't smoke; lying there half covered in the mud he had crawled through to get ashore from the boat, there was no danger of anyone smelling him

Here, on the outside of the island, away from the channel, there was little sign of human life ever having been there. There was no sign of discarded fishing line, beach fires used to cook the fishermen's food, empty cigarette packets or dropped matches. Nothing except the now sparse wild rice, the only remaining evidence of a 1930's attempt to introduce agriculture to these off-shore islands. He stood up slowly, scanning the horizon with his night glasses from this higher position.

To his left and on the other side of the island, a group of lights indicated the position of the defence post established by the People's Army. Pressure lamps, he couldn't hear them hissing from here but he knew that they would be and that that would mask any slight sounds that he made in approaching their camp of three wooden huts. There wouldn't be much to report on this island, he thought. Probably just a defended observation post which would report the arrival of any vessel trying to enter the channel.

He moved forward slowly, silently and constantly watching for any sign of life; a soldier who had left the camp to relieve himself, a camp cook discarding soil or scraps outside the perimeter of the little group of huts so that the inevitable rats would not enter the camp itself.

Owens disliked rats. He wasn't afraid of them or anything like that, indeed they represented a potentially valuable source of protein but he didn't like them. A friend, working alone in Malaya, had been forced to take shelter under what cover there had been on a river bank and had been bitten by a rat that had regarded him as an intruder. By the time he had come out of the jungle, the leg had been so badly infected that it had had to be amputated, leaving him with just one leg and no career prospects in the Royal Marines; certainly not in the commandos.

Owens hoped that he wouldn't end up like that. Getting shot was an occupational hazard, even being killed less pleasantly or more slowly was an acceptable risk in this profession but to be crippled by a rat bite was no way for an officer and a gentleman to be discharged from the service.

A nesting bird flew into the air with a cry as he stepped too close to its nest. He froze, stooping to reduce his silhouette should anyone look to see what had disturbed it. He doubted that anyone would; ground birds' nests were subject to attack by marauding rats looking for eggs and the chances were that any soldier detailed for duty on an island like this would be an uneducated country boy who would know such things. The salt of the earth in anybody's army, slow witted but reliable soldiers who could be trusted to stand on guard duty for hours, watching and seeing nothing but constantly aware of what was going on around them. No, the bird's cry would not alarm any sentry on duty on the island, only a city boy, unused to the silence of the night, would be consciously aware of it and wonder if it was worth investigating.

The three huts of rough, un-planed wooden planks, stood on the highest part of the island and, in front of them, three howitzers stood, soldier-like, facing out to sea. Even to Owens, it was obvious that the ground here was too soft to support the concrete platforms required to mount heavy artillery; that would be on the main island of Wolmi and, perhaps on some of the other, larger islands closer to the shore to provide a covering of cross fire against any ship silly enough to try and force a passage between them.

He worked his way around the encampment to make sure that there were no more guns that he couldn't see from here and to locate the ammunition boxes which would tell him how much ammunition this offshore island had been given. He didn't expect to find very much.

Any warship trying to enter the channel and resisted by this exposed and tiny artillery emplacement would quickly and efficiently destroy it. There wouldn't be much ammunition here, the soldier's job was to keep watch and to warn the big guns of an approaching target. They would be expected to fire a few rounds at the incoming vessel in the hope of a lucky shot and then to run away until the danger had passed.

The small stack of boxes confirmed his assumption and, satisfied that there was nothing more to see, he followed the shoreline round to the other end of the island and assessed the best way to get across to the next.

By any reasonable assessment, his objective was too far for him to swim before daylight left him exposed to any watchers. He dug a slight depression in the soft ground behind a bush and, tearing one or two branches from nearby bushes, crawled into his hide and pulled the extra cover in behind him.

Satisfied that he wouldn't be seen unless someone actually stumbled upon him, he pressed the Record button on his radio and dictated the encoded position and strength of the first obstacle to any landing using the Flying Fish Channel. Also important to this survey was the position and strength of any emplacement covering an approach across the shallow waters either side of the channel, the route that would be taken by approaching landing craft making for the shore at high tide; he pressed Transmit.

At low tide, the mud flats extended for more than a mile out from the low shore where a sea wall had been built many years ago. He would have a look at that too, if the opportunity presented itself; see what was on the other side of the wall that might deter a landing.

On this island, there was only the one gun position and that faced the channel which was reasonable as it was the most seaward look out position. Further in, he expected to find bigger, better placed and more seriously armed emplacements. Tomorrow. For tonight, he would sleep where he was, it was reasonably warm, dry and he was in no immediate danger of discovery. It occurred to him to hope that there weren't any dogs on the island.

* * *

The beach below Camp Xray was almost covered with landing craft. The big LST's that would take the tanks and trucks to wherever they were going and now, a fleet of LCP's, Landing Craft Personnel, was being gathered. These were the smaller landing craft which would be used to transport the marines and soldiers ashore from the troop transports. God help the sailors who manned those little boats, they steered like shoe boxes even in calm water.

Anchored off-shore was the giant LSI. Underpowered and with only the most basic and uncomfortable accommodation for their crews and the crews of the smaller landing craft that she carried, she would have trouble sailing any great distance so, Sergeant Thomas deduced, the landing was to be not too far up the coast, probably Kunsan or somewhere like that. If the intended landing zone had been on the east coast, Camp

Xray wouldn't have been built here. No, it would have to be the west coast, he was sure of that.

None of this deduction was of any use to Sergeant Thomas except as a means of winning any bet he could get any fool to take on. Sergeant Thomas had been in the Marines for seven years, had taken part in more landings than he chose to remember and the site of every one of them had been the subject of much betting by the waiting men. Over the years, as experience taught him the way officers thought, his ability to outguess the other men had grown and by the end of the war, had allowed him to make some quite considerable wins.

It was some years now though, since the end of that war, and this present bunch of privates had been just kids when Thomas had learned how to predict the future. He was a happy man. He would make a lot of money out of this war and, as a cook, was reasonably certain that he would survive it. This wasn't going to be like the last war, chasing Japanese soldiers from tree to tree, each one sworn to defend the Emperor to the death; his death, of course, not the Emperor's. Thomas was a republican, he didn't believe in Emperors. At least, this time, the enemy was a bunch of Commies who should have been grateful to be freed from Japanese occupation by the Americans.

Thomas's knowledge of the political situation in post-war Korea was limited and incomplete. In the north of the Korean peninsular, the Japanese had surrendered to the Russians although the Russians had only declared war on Japan after the Americans had defeated them elsewhere. There had been no serious fighting; the Emperor had told the Japanese army to surrender and the army had, very largely, obeyed that order; it was just unfortunate for Sergeant Thomas and all the other poor souls here now that the Russians had been the nearest army to which they could surrender.

The Russians, moving south from their own border, had invaded Korea more to prevent the Chinese from doing so than from any premeditated anti-American plan. China had, at least in theory, still been governed by Chiang kai-shek then and Russia had long supported the interests of Mao and his communists who had been fighting both the Japanese and, surreptitiously, the Chinese Government at the same time.

Sergeant Thomas didn't know that and that lack of essential intelligence could just result in his being caught in a fire fight between the US Marines and a well trained, well armed and politically motivated North Korean army hell bent on taking over the entire Korean peninsular and re-uniting the country under a Socialist government.

He might very well win his bets on the location of the landing and die a rich man but whilst to die a rich man might be every American's ambition, Sergeant Thomas had no desire to die just yet. He would use every trick he had learned in his wartime progress across the Pacific, hopping from island to island and with anything like reasonable luck, he would survive this war too.

He shouted at a private who was walking past the cookhouse with his hands in his pockets. Soldiers? These kids didn't know what soldiering was about but, they were about to find out. Yes Siree!

TWELVE

"Challenger should be back by tomorrow afternoon Sir. Will you want to brief her Captain on arrival?"

"Thank you Flags   No. Let them have a run ashore first then we zapp 'em with the good news; that they are going straight back out again. Have you their instructions ready? I don't want any misunderstandings on this one, too many Americans involved for comfort and you know how their top brass screams if anything goes wrong, particularly if they can blame it on someone else. At least Powers can't complain about being bored doing routine patrols up north."

Admiral Dickenson was worried about this feint landing. He suspected that he had drawn the short straw though he hadn't been invited to make any choice at all. In seven days, Challenger and an American ship were to put ashore a large body of US Marines and a smaller number of Royals. This landing, together with numerous others all along both the east and the west coasts were designed to destabilise the enemy.

Challenger's landing at Ch'onan, wasn't actually on the coast but there was a convenient tidal creek that led to within a few miles of this important inland road junction and the defence of this would draw north Korean troops south from the proposed real invasion site further north, at Inchon.

It had all been carefully timed. These feint landings must be big enough to attract the attention of the enemy. troops They had to be held for long enough to give the enemy time to recognise that they were being attached by multiple landings along the coast and to move their reinforcements south to deal with them. Only thus, it was reasoned, could there be any real chance of getting the main invasion ashore at Inchon without unacceptable losses.

Inchon had two advantages; he had to admit that. One, it was a major port and this would permit the rapid dispersal of men and materials once taken and two, that it was very close to Seoul, the capital of South Korea and therefore vastly symbolic. If Seoul could be retaken quickly, together with its nearby major airport, the invasion would be safe and politically significant. It would put heart into the South's fledgling army and that, in turn, would save a great many British and American lives.

Second Officer Archer, Daphne to both the admiral and his flag lieutenant Terry Bowden, placed the cup of strong black coffee on the admiral's desk and the signal sheet into his outstretched hand.

"Thank you. Chalk these new positions on the chart will you."

Bowden took the signal and placed it on the big chart table in his own office; the relevant chart was already laid out on view.

"How long can Owens keep this up, do you think?"

Daphne stood, watching the flag lieutenant marking on the chart the positions of two more gun emplacements and noting the number and calibre of the guns emplaced.

"God knows. He should have starved to death by now, even if he hasn't been shot."

"I don't think I could marry a man who's idea of a good idea is doing what lieutenant Qwens is doing."

"Is that what you want? A man to marry?"

"God no! I didn't mean it like that. I meant that if I was asked by a man like that, I don't think I could marry him. I don't think I could stand the stain of not knowing what he was up to nor where."

Lieutenant Bowden made a mental note not to volunteer for commando training. He wasn't sure just what his intentions were towards Daphne Archer but he liked her a lot and he had a shrewd idea that she had got his number.

Dickenson had, on his desk five other reports from Lieutenant Owen; he was very pleased with this little operation. Quietly and without the enemy knowing he was there, Owens had managed so far to visit most of the islands. He had reported no problems and seemed to be in good spirits. Good man, Owens. One of these days, he must ask him how he managed to live off the land when there was hardly any land there to live off and how he managed to get from island to island but that would keep.

The position and strength of all the defence positions Owens had found were being marked on a chart locked in the Admiral's safe. He had another seven days before he would present this intelligence to MacArthur; inviting him to share it with the captain's of all the ships that would be attempting the landing at Inchon. He would make sure that all the British Captains had this information, the rest was up to MacArthur.

* * *

The channel narrowed as Challenger steamed slowly in from the sea. Sasebo was on her port side and, as she came up to the position indicated for her anchorage, Lieutenant Chas Turner stood on the Foc's'le with his Foc's'le party, ready to knock off the clip and let the anchor run out. Standing astride the bullring in the eye of the ship, Signalman Martin had one foot on either side of the Jack Staff at the top of which, rolled and snagged for breaking, the Union flag hung.

When the Blakes Slip was knocked off, releasing the anchor chain, a single light tug by Martin on the halyard would break the binding on the rolled and tied Union flag. Its instant display would indicate to all the other ships, and the Admirals Flag Lieutenant who would be watching, that Challenger was anchored. This would, in turn, result in the ship's identification pennants being lowered from the starboard yardarm and the dismissal of the foc's'le party and the Special Sea Dutymen who had been closed up at their stations in case of emergency since entering the channel.

On the bridge, the captain relaxed. "Finished with engines, Number One. I think it's about lunchtime and I'm hungry."

"Very good Sir." He leaned over the voice pipe in front of him. "Wheelhouse. Finished with engines. Pipe, Stand down Special Sea Dutymen, open all X and Y openings and Up Spirits, Leading Hands of the Mess to muster for rum. You can pipe Hands to Dinner in twenty minutes."

From the wheelhouse, the Coxswain repeated the orders and confirmed that the Engine room had repeated back Finished with engines. Throughout the ship, men returned to their normal places of harbour employment and the Coxswain went below to issue the rum.

"OK Martin?" The Yeoman handed the Signalman of the watch a clean white ensign. "Go and change the ensign. That one's too frayed to leave it up in harbour. We may be at war again but we can't have the ship flying a dirty, frayed ensign in harbour. Got to show off a bit, ain't we."

"If you say so, Yeo."

Signalman Martin was not surprised to be given the clean white ensign. War or no war, the Royal Navy wore a clean ensign in harbour. It was Martin's opinion that, had the admiralty not been too mean to pay for them, the yeoman in every ship in the fleet would insist on flying clean, new ensigns at all times. Show the flag, that was what the navy was about. Show the wogs that the Royal Navy was here.

THIRTEEN

Lieutenant Owen smelled. This was, in itself, a good thing, it would help hide him amongst the many smells of the foliage from amongst which he peered at the huge gun emplacement in front of him. How had they got anything that big on to the island? Must be at least 100mm.

Big and therefore dangerous, these guns could make short work of any destroyer that came within range, let alone anything as vulnerable as a troopship full of soldiers; troopships weren't designed to be shot at.

Owen buried himself deeper into the foliage, scooping out an indentation into which he could sink further out of possible sight of any sentry who wasted his time looking inland rather than out to sea. He had had a near thing earlier that morning when a sentry, unable to wait for his relief to arrive, had checked that his officers were not paying attention to what he was doing and had sneaked into the low scrubby bushes to squat and relieve himself.

Owens was grateful for the smell that he had acquired in the ten days he had been ashore; the young soldier had not noticed that he was taking a shit less than two metres from a Royal Marine Lieutenant. He wondered what the boy would have thought of had that Royal Marine Lieutenant had to slit his throat to ensure his silence. Of course, that would have meant spiriting the boy's body away so that there would be no indication of his own presence on the island; he would have had to risk moving in daylight so that, when the boy's relief did arrive and found him gone, the inevitable search would find nothing.

He had been lucky. The boy had not seen him. He had relieved himself, wiped himself with his hand and then wiped that on the foliage of the scrub bushes amongst which Owens was hiding.

Three more days of this and he could go to ground somewhere safer and wait to be picked up. Two more islands to check; he hoped that they were not as well armed as this one. Ideally, they would be unarmed, uninhabited and uninteresting other than as a safe hole in which to hide himself until he could get away.

The guards were being relieved. He could see the officer detailing the soldiers for their various posts and no doubt telling them how important it was that they keep a good lookout. They, like all young soldiers on guard duties, would nod obediently and go to their posts convinced that like all officers, theirs was quite mad. Who could they be guarding the island against? The Americans and the South Korean army had run away,

They were here, on this elevated mud flat, guarding two bloody great guns from the fishes and the sea birds; no one else came near it. The local fishermen had been warned off on pain of being shot for target practice and the enemy didn't even know they were here. There was no danger, nothing to guard against, no need to pay too much attention to keeping a lookout.

In half an hour or so, the Sergeant would come round to make sure that they were awake and not playing cards or drinking illegally imported beer; some of the more enterprising local fishermen were not above doing a little trade with the soldiers from the other side of the island after dark.

Owens, his own observations completed and the new guards now safely bored with looking round a sea with nothing on it and an island with very little more, slid slowly backwards out of the hide-hole he had made and crawled away, making use of every possible piece of cover. It wouldn't be safe to stay that close to the gun emplacement for a whole day, you could never be sure when one of the officers or sergeants would become bored enough to take a walk; anything to break the boredom of their life.

This was better. He had regained the denser thicket in which he had spent the night, waiting for the daylight to show him whatever there was to see on this new island. He had not expected to find such a major emplacement this far up the main channel; there must be a reason for it but for the moment, it escaped him. This island and the channel near which it sat, could be swept by gunfire from the larger mainland shore batteries; there seemed no apparent reason for the placing of such big guns here.

In this shallow sea of constantly changing mud banks and tide races, it could be that another useable channel had opened up or even that the main channel, not dredged for some months now had silted up and a new channel been formed by the diverted waters. He would check that.

He swept the limited horizon again, slowly moving his binoculars, carefully holding each picture framed for a moment or more so that any movement would be apparent. This half of the island was deserted, except for the gun emplacement, its accompanying wooden hutted barrack and him and he hoped that nobody knew that he was there.

The small transceiver clicked on and he dictated his position and that of the gun emplacement together with its details into the tiny tape recorder built into the machine. His message completed, he pressed 'transmit' and, in less than a minute,

117

his message had been transmitted with no fear of its being picked up by the enemy and his position located. Let head quarters sort out what to do about the big guns, it wasn't his job; his job was to locate them and report them. He imagined that the airplane jockeys would do something about them before the landings began or perhaps, to prevent any attack being read as a warning by the enemy, simultaneously with the start of the invasion.

* * *

At Camp Xray, Sergeant cook Thomas recognised the signs. Departure could not be long delayed; in his years in the Marine Corps, he had seen it many times, the setting up of a temporary encampment followed by its removal, its purpose served.

The tanks had all been tested, the trucks had been tested, the heavy guns, heavy that is by marine standards, had been tested and they had all been protected against water ingress by being covered over with grease and camouflaged tarps.

There they sat, silently, within the giant LCT's, waiting for the off; waiting for their war to start. The mechanics and armourers had done all that they could, now it was down to the fighting men to do what they had been trained to do. He had laid his bets with the greenhorns at the camp. His money said that the landing would be at Kunsan; he would go home a rich man.

In the tents, spread out over the area of the camp, young marines and soldiers cleaned and checked their small arms, they knew it couldn't be long now. Everything was ready, they were waiting for the green light from the top brass in Tokyo. It would be tough, they all knew that. The enemy was not only fighting in what it believed to be its own country but had been successful for so long now that its morale was high.

They had driven the under trained South Korean army a hundred and eighty miles in front of them, killing, capturing and in many instances, recycling them as good communists, happy to be on what they now believed to be the winning side.

The Yanks! They were not afraid of the Americans. They too had been forced to retire in front of the power of the People's army; nothing could stop them now from driving the interfering Americans into the sea of the Korea Strait and unifying Korea as a single, Socialist State; The People's Republic of Korea.

The dogs were still here or perhaps they were different dogs, he couldn't tell and didn't really care. They were hanging round the cookhouse, on the lookout for any morsel that might be discarded by these strangers who seemed so well provided for. Whilst the dogs could smell the difference between the native Koreans and these foreigners, the nationality of the provider was immaterial; food was food and they would lick any hand that fed them.

The loudspeakers throughout the camp burst into life. "Now hear this, now hear this. 'A', 'B' and 'C' companies to muster on the parade ground with full kit 'D' and 'E' companies will muster in one hour. The smoking lamp is out."

Marines and soldiers tumbled from their tents carrying their kit, making for the parade ground. Everything but their personal arms would be taken from them and transported separately; to be landed when the beachhead had been established. Until then, they would need nothing but their guns and as much ammunition as they could carry. Their job was to get ashore and establish a beachhead big enough for the big transports to beach and off-load their trucks and the thousand and one things they would need to maintain and expand the beachhead into the surrounding countryside wherever they landed. So far, nobody had told them where it would be.

The tanks would be coming ashore with them, blasting their way up from the beach into whatever lay behind it and once there, to fan out and give protection to the foot soldiers who would be doing most of the shooting and killing.

The first three companies were assembled, checked, inspected and ferried out to the waiting troop transports. The big, landingcraft-carrying, USS Comstock had already left, taking the small landing craft which would be in position, ready to receive and land the troops when the troop carriers arrived.

The LST's were still in sight but well out to sea, heading for the rendezvous from which the landings would be made. There, navy ships would be in attendance, shepherding them into position, protecting them from air attack and the big cruisers and even perhaps the Battleship the Might Mo would be standing further off-shore ready to begin the barrage of heavy gunfire that would punch a hole through any defences there might be immediately behind the beach.

This creeping barrage would progressively destroy anything standing in their way, the huge high explosive shells together with bombs from carrier based aircraft destroying any building or gun emplacement that stood between the marines and their beachhead. It would, hopefully, simultaneously detonate any land mines within reach of the explosions; piece of cake, as the Limeys always said, the landing would probably be unopposed anyway, the enemy didn't know they were coming. Yeah, a piece of cake; they had to believe that.

Sergeant Thomas smiled to himself. He wouldn't be going ashore with the first wave; that was for the fighting men. He would be in the third wave, following up the fighting men with hot food as they rotated from the front line, exhausted, dirty and hungry; it had always been like that. War was a dirty business in every respect. Any soldier going into battle would be bathed in his own sweat to which dust and dirt would stick, making him look worse than he actually felt. And any soldier who had done this before, knew enough to make himself look worse than he was. It was a form of camouflage, not only against the enemy but against his own Sergeant who, whilst demanding spotless appearance on the parade ground, expected his men to be mud covered and exhausted in battle.

* * *

Lieutenant Terrance Bowden, the Admiral's Flag Lieutenant knocked on the door and entered the office. He handed the signal to the admiral without comment.

"Nice one Flags. That just about covers all the islands."

"Yes Sir. Incredible, isn't it. I mean, how the hell does he flit gaily from island to island spying on their defences without anybody noticing him?"

"It probably has something to do with his being bloody good at it, Flags. OK, make the latest alterations to the charts and then organise a flight to Tokyo. You may have the honour of delivering them to MacArthur and Admiral Joy. I shall remain here out of harm's way.

"They will probably explode when you give them this information which they should have had the foresight to arrange for themselves so it will be safer if I stay here, then you can claim no responsibility whatever.

" Unless they reintroduce the custom of killing the messenger, I should be safe enough."

" The important thing is to ensure that Admiral Joy recognises the importance of this intelligence, it's his ships and mine that will have to deal with these emplacements before the troopships can even attempt to enter the harbour. The landings can get ashore without going through the Flying Fish Channel but once they have taken the port from the landward, we must be ready to take the supplies and additional troops directly into Inchon at the next high tide. The whole thing depends upon getting the maximum possible number of troops and equipment ashore as quickly as possible and retaking Seoul before the communists can do anything about it.

"Before you do the chart amendments, ask Daphne to come in will you."

The Flag Lieutenant found her making a cup of coffee for the Admiral, he told her she was wanted.

"Daphne, how kind of you." The admiral smiled at her as she put the cup of coffee on his desk. "A little job for you. I want to see Commander Powers of Challenger, see if you can get hold of him will you. It's a bit urgent."

She left him stirring the coffee and looking out of the window. She wondered what he had in mind for David Powers and Challenger that was becoming a kind of private ship, a detached command, doing little jobs for the admiral rather than acting as part of the Eighth Destroyer Flotilla under Captain D in Cossack.

David had better make good and sure that he had specific orders from the admiral or his Captain D could accuse him of swanning off on these little jaunts and leaving the rest of the Flotilla to do all the essential but boring work. That wouldn't do his career any good; his future depended upon a good write-up from Captain D. She made a mental note to ensure that his orders were copied, for information, to Captain D if the admiral didn't do it himself. Strictly speaking, his flag lieutenant should do that, cross the T's and dot the I's, that is what flag lieutenant's are for.

It was almost two weeks since she and Terry Bowden had had their dinner ashore and she had been waiting for his next move. If he didn't make it soon, she would have to assume that he wasn't going to make one. She knew that he had been busy, so had she, they both worked for the same admiral but he should have said or done something by now.

For a moment, she had wondered if she had ruined her chances with him when she had mentioned marriage in relation to Lieutenant Owen; he had certainly reacted to the word marry, she would have to nudge him along a bit.

Lieutenant Bowden came back from his office, a roll of charts under his arm. "I've got to go to Tokyo for the admiral. I've put it in hand for tomorrow, I don't suppose you'd like to come too?"

"And what, Lieutenant Bowden, would himself say if we both swanned off to Tokyo?"

"Actually, he suggested it and anyway, I shall need some protection from the wrath of God, MacArthur that is, when he discovers that we have jeopardised his whole Inchon landing plan by having young Owens flitting from island to island in the Flying fish Channel gathering intelligence; he could go ape. If Owens had been captured, he would have talked, everyone does you know and then MacArthur's plan would have backfired disastrously, we would have been landing against a prepared enemy shore. The losses would have been unimaginable."

"And himself is sending you with the message I take it and just in case they threaten to kill the messenger, I'm to provide you with your dying wish; is that it?"

"Something like that, I hope. I don't mean that I hope I die, I mean that I hope you'll come."

Perhaps she wouldn't have to nudge too hard after all.

FOURTEEN

Challenger laid to her anchor in Sasebo for three further leave-less days, refuelling, restoring and generally pretending to be busy whilst, one by one, the hardworking frigates entered the port; Cardigan Bay, Morecombe Bay, Whitesand Bay, Brides Bay and Mounts Bay. In turn, each of these worn, World War Two, sea-going workhorses refuelled and rearmed, took on food and water and prepared for their return to sea.

"Something must be up Number One, something is definitely up; I wonder if we're involved?"

*   *   *

"There's a Mr Browning to see you Sir." Second Officer Archer passed the man's card to the admiral. "An American. He said you were expecting him."

The questioning tone in her voice made it quite clear that she didn't believe what the man had said and that she didn't like the look of him.

"Ask him to come in please Daphne. I imagine he must be the American I was asked to see."

She stood aside as the brash young American strode past her and into the admiral's office.

"Glad to see you Admiral, my name's Browning, CIA. I was told you would be expecting me but your secretary here seems unaware of my business with you." He placed his briefcase on the admiral's desk and stood as if expecting the admiral to stand to attention and give him a welcoming address.

"Thank you Daphne. Perhaps you would ask my Flag Lieutenant to join us. No, don't bother with refreshments, Mr Browning won't be here for long."

Admiral Dickenson remained seated and looked at his visitor over the top of the card that he held in front of him as if he was having difficulty reading it.

"I won't keep you a minute Mr Browning, my Flag Lieutenant is no doubt making his excuses to the Fleet Commander with whom he had an appointment for this time."

Browning glanced around him at the office. Not up to an American Admiral's standard but he was relieved to see the two comfortable looking easy chairs and the coffee table upon which was displayed a highly polished and empty brass ashtray. He wanted a cigarette but had the feeling that he had better not light one, that he had not made a very good impression on this Limey Admiral. God, he hated these pumped up Europeans who thought still that they, not the Americans ruled the world.

"Ah, here you are. Flags, Mr Browning, may I introduce my Flag Lieutenant, Lieutenant Bowden. Flags, Mr Bowden I hope bears a message from Lieutenant Colonel Kramer. Lieutenant Colonel Kramer, you will remember, heads up the CIA in this theatre and is most desirous of our cooperation in a little clandestine operation he has in mind."

Left standing in front of the admiral's desk like some office boy sent to see his Chairman, Browning confirmed to himself that he didn't like Europeans and particularly, he didn't like stuck up Limey Admirals.

The admiral, satisfied that he had made clear their relative positions in the pecking order, smiled at Browning. "Perhaps you'd like to put your satchel on the coffee table Mr Browning; we can sit more comfortably there, don't you think? Flags, pull up one of those spare chairs, will you. You may want to make a note or two. Now Mr Browning, what exactly is it that my old friend 'Dutch' Kramer would like from me?"

* * *

Cossack stood off shore, roughly on a line with the thirty eighth parallel, Captain D8 now had his patrols nicely under control. Had he been asked, he would have had to admit that at first it had all been a bit hit and miss. With ships being drawn from so many navies, it had taken some time to get organised but now order reigned in his multi-national command. He was annoyed that the half-leader of his Flotilla, Challenger, seemed to have been again co-opted by the CinC but that's the navy, if he couldn't take a joke he shouldn't have joined; he would get his own back later. When Challenger returned, Commander David Powers would find himself busier than he had ever been in his life and Cossack would take a long break in Japan for what the Americans called Rest and Recreation.

His present position, thirty miles to seaward of Paengnyong-do, allowed him to run south, into South Korean waters or, north into North Korean territory as required to offer support to any of his ships that required a little extra firepower.

He had lost all his Frigates, sent for by CinC for some reason and the destroyer Constance had been sent south for repairs after getting a little too close to the shore and being holed just above the water line by shore fire; a totally unexpected 100mm gun emplacement but on the whole, he was happy with the state of affairs.

The enemy, were getting too many of these big guns for comfort and as they were coming in from Russia on North Korea's north east border, stopping their entry was the responsibility of the Yanks. They would be coming down the east coast railway and then moved across by land to the west coast where they were shooting at his ships.

Off the north east coast, he knew that the bigger, American ships were shooting up anything that moved but he would have to report that the number of heavy guns on the west coast was increasing. More air raids, he supposed; it was the only way to attack anything moving more than a few miles from the coast.

*　*　*

Challenger left Sasebo at one o-clock in the morning, taking advantage of the low cloud cover and lack of moonlight to cover her departure.

"Well Sir, Off again, eh? Back to the old stamping ground?"

"No Number One, not yet. Seems CinC has another of his 'little jobs' he wants done first. We're to join up with the USS Eustace A. Bart for a bit of landing party support. She's one of their old destroyers; perfect for the east coast but too deep draught for this job."

"The only Bart I ever heard of was some kind of Peer and unlikely to be an American Sir. I don't think I've ever heard of her."

"No, well, you shouldn't have, nor should anybody else. They've been busy modifying her for just this kind of work. All cloak and dagger stuff."

"Do we know what and where, Sir?"

"Yes and no in that order Harry. No doubt they'll tell us all about it when we meet tomorrow night. We should meet them in the early hours of the morning, I can only hope they have their recognition signals all organised 'cos I ain't stopping for anyone else; not even if we meet Captain D. Boss's orders! We're working with the Spooks this time so stand by for a real cowboy's pantomime."

"Sorry Sir. Spooks?"

"CIA. They're a bit new. Used to be the OSS but Truman

closed them down at the end of the war and formed this new agency called the Central Intelligence Agency. Don't know why but that's what Presidents do, I suppose. Put their own marker on things, as it were."

"Ah, I have heard of them, I think. Something that Royal said when we had him aboard. He'd worked with them, I think. I rather gathered that they were into inserting spies into the north but not having much luck as far as I could gather. Seems half the South Koreans they recruited turned their coats as soon as they'd been landed north of the border. Probably back in the south by now, as spies for the other lot!"

"Oh what a tangled web we weave, eh Harry? Hope they haven't told the other side that we're coming.

"OK Number One. Fall out Special Sea Dutymen but leave X and Y openings closed, just in case some sneak has mined the channel between here and Nakadori-Shima. Go to Defence Stations in two hours, eh?"

"Very good, Sir."

He repeated the orders into the voice pipe to the wheelhouse where the Coxswain broadcast them throughout the ship.

"Bridge, Wheelhouse. Leading Seaman Charles on the wheel Sir."

"Very good. Tell the Cox'n we'll be going to Defence Stations in two hours."

*   *   *

Captain D8's Chief Yeoman of Signals handed him the clipboard. He hadn't heard him knock on the door, must be getting old and deaf or, more likely, too busy thinking about something else. He must watch that.

Consort had spotted a number of small craft, patrol boats, junks and others of unspecified nature attempting a landing on the island of Taewha-do and had engaged. She had come

Challenger's War

under fire from a shore battery that they hadn't spotted before; probably hadn't been there until a day or two ago!

Three armed junks, and a number of sampans carrying troops had been sunk but the two escorting North Korean fast patrol boats had used their power to escape into a fog bank under cover or which they had hoped to succeed in landing their troops on the island.

Whilst that particular island was not of any particular strategic value, there were a few South Korean forces on it, just to establish proprietorial rights and for it to have been captured without his ship's knowing, would have allowed the North Koreans to mount heavy guns on it and do a great deal of damage to the next patrolling destroyer.

"Thank you Chief Yeoman. Ask the First Lieutenant to see me, would you."

He walked over to the plan chest and withdrew the appropriate chart.

"You wanted me Sir?"

"Ah, Number One. We may have a small problem on Taewha-do. Consort has reported an attempted landing by NKPA troops but he's not sure how many, if any, actually got ashore before he shot up their transports. I suppose it's inevitable that some of them got ashore, even if the had to swim for it and if enough of them managed it, the ROK garrison may be overwhelmed. Can't afford to have them building gun emplacements on the offshore islands, can we. It would make our inshore patrols altogether too risky."

"We could send one of the sloops down there to take a look, get a few armed men ashore to do a reci."

"Ask my Secretary to pop up, will you? I think we need to do something pretty quickly then advise CinC that the People's Army is getting ambitious. He can tell the South Korean people and they can send some more troops up to get their island back if its been lost and strengthen the garrison if it hasn't.

* * *

In Consort, the mood was perhaps not as up-beat as it might have been had they been sure that they had got all the boats before anyone got ashore.

"What do you think, Guns? Did we get 'em all?"

"Doubt it Sir. Too many and with the fog drifting about like that, there's no way to know how many there were. Still, we've told Capt. D and no doubt he will advise. "

"Well, I'm not going any closer to the island until I know whether they had any big guns and whether they are now in the hands of the People's Army."

He turned to the voice pipe beside his chair. "Plot, Bridge. Pilot, give me a course for clear water will you, I'm not going to risk getting caught between that shore battery and anything they might have on the island."

"Steer 290 Sir. That'll get us out of range of both quite quickly. Fast as you like Sir."

"Thank you Pilot. Wheelhouse, Bridge. Port fifteen." He watched giro repeater under the forebridge canopy tick round as the ship's head moved to port. "Meet her Cox'n, steer two nine zero."

"Course 290, Sir."

"We were lucky not to have been hit ourselves from the shore Sir, don't you think?"

"Yes Guns and I don't intend pushing my luck any further this afternoon."

* * *

Captain D's Secretary stood in the doorway, his hat under his arm.

"Come in Brian. We need to send someone to take a look at this island, Taewha-do. Bit of a kerfuffle there this afternoon.

Consort says she interrupted an invasion by the other side but isn't sure if anyone got ashore. Don't want to risk any of the Destroyers so we'll send one of the sloops, they can get in close and send a boat ashore. Do a bit of snooping. Who's nearest?"

"Probably Opossum Sir."

"How appropriate. OK, I'll have her go down there and send a boat in. She can lie possum just out of sight till the boat gets back.

"Ah, Chief Yeoman. Have this encrypted and sent to Opossum, quick as you can, eh? Mark it Immediate. Proceed to Taewha-do where North Korean army may have landed troops. Investigate but don't put ship at risk. Rendezvous with Consort to west of island and cooperate. Then, send this signal to Consort. Opossum will rendezvous west of Taewha-do to assist in investigation of reported landing. Make that Immediate too. OK?"

"On their way, Sir."

"What do you think, Sir? Real trouble?"

"Well Schooly," the Captain D's secretary was always one of the young lieutenants with pale blue between the rank rings on his sleeve, an Education Officer. "Probably not too serious but if the other side get established on the off-shore islands then we won't be able to send our ships close enough inshore to do and damage to their railways, etc. With luck, the South Korean army will send some reinforcements up there but we need to be a little careful for a few days, until we see just what we are up against."

"I hope they tell us they're sending their men up. Consort is perfectly capable of sinking anything she sees if they don't give the proper recognition signal."

"Are you suggesting that Consort's captain is trigger-happy Schooly?"

"Not for a moment Sir."

"Good but you'd better make sure that he is warned."

"Of course, Sir. How long do you think this is going to last, sir?"

"What?"

"This war, Sir."

"Why, have you something better to do?"

"I had rather hoped to go back to Cambridge sir. After my national service of course."

"And so you shall, Schooly; just as soon as we win this war."

FIFTEEN

Challenger found the American Destroyer exactly where she was supposed to be, blacked out and at action stations just in case the radar contact she had been tracking for the last two hours was not who she hoped it would be. Recognition signals exchanged, Challenger stopped and lowered her 'skimming dish' motorboat, the Captain's favourite toy.

At only sixteen feet, it was too small for work if any kind of a sea was running but fast and fun in harbour or if the conditions made its use possible elsewhere. This, he had decided, was a perfect opportunity to show off to the Yank captain and, he had to admit even to himself, there weren't many opportunities nowadays to do that.

Captain Masters met him at the gangway as he climbed up the short rope ladder that had been let down for him.

"Nice to see you Commander. Welcome aboard the USS Eustace A. Bart. Now ain't that one hell of a name for an itsy bitsy little boat like this? Never mind, she'll do for this kind of work. Can't drive around in a hulking great battleship and hope not to be noticed can we? Sorry but this is the US Navy so there's no chance of a drink but there's coffee in plenty in my cabin.

"Like your speedboat Commander, now how do I get me one of those?"

"Well, Captain, much as I am pleased to cooperate with the US Navy, I wouldn't recommend that you try to steal my boat. My Coxswain has taken an almost proprietary interest in her and, so have I. We don't get to carry very many toys in the RN and my Skimming Dish is probably the only fun thing we do carry."

"Don't panic Commander, I won't pull rank on you in that. Now, do you take cream and sugar in your coffee?"

The USS Eustace A. Bart had once been an ordinary USN destroyer, one of the hundreds of so called tin cans built during World War Two but since her adoption by the recently formed Central Intelligence Agency, had undergone considerable specialised modification.

Initially, her entire after superstructure had been removed, together with the guns that that had supported. Forward of this superstructure, the torpedo tubes had also been removed and the considerable deck space released by this denudation now supported a large crane located between and designed to load or unload the four LCP landing craft suspended in two two-tier davits.

On what had originally been the quarterdeck, the depth charge throwers and racks had given way to a specially adapted mounting for a small but businesslike scout helicopter.

Petty Officer George Martin, Challenger's Coxswain and self appointed driver of the Skimming Dish stood taking in the modifications made to the American ship.

"They don't make many like this, do they! "

The American Petty Officer looking after him looked for'ard and aft before answering. "There ain't no more like this beast. She's special."

"Yeah. I can see that. With all this extra top hamper, why doesn't she just roll over in the first puff of wind?"

"We're deeper in the water than she used to be; ballast. The reduced freeboard makes it easier to launch the landing craft so it all worked out pretty well. Have to admit though, she's a bastard in a heavy sea and she ain't much to look at; not pretty like she used to be."

"You always been a destroyer man?"

"Yeah. Didn't get on in the big ships; too many officers."

"Yeah, I know the feeling. Spent most of my time in destroyers and frigates. Sort of special kind of navy ain't it; not like the spit and polish navy in the big ships."

"You said it Buddy. How long's your Old Man gonna be aboard?"

"No idea. As long as it takes for yours to brief him on whatever we're going to do. Any idea what that is?"

"Yeah, s'pose its safe enough to tell you now. You won't have a chance to tell the enemy. We're loaded to the gun'ls with Special Forces personnel; we've even got some of yours aboard. We're to land them up some creek north of here and they're to capture some hick town with an important road junction. The way I heard it, they have to capture this place, hold it for a few days and then get the hell out of there back to the ship."

"Oh, nothing serious then."

"Na. Your Marine Commandos reckon it'll be a piece of cake. If they reckon getting their arses shot off is a piece of cake, they must be fucking mad but I guess that's the primary qualification for joining an outfit like theirs, eh?"

"Rather them than me, mate."

"Come below. There's coffee in the mess. The Quartermaster will give us a shout when your man's ready to leave." He led the way forward through the break door into the foc'sle.

In the Captain's cabin, Commander Powers looked at the chart laid out on the table. "The idea is Commander, we drop our landing craft as close inshore as we can get and, you being shallower draught than we are now, you escort them into the creek and take out any shore batteries that might get in their way. We've got a hundred and fifty of our Marine Special Forces aboard and fifty of yours.

"All they have to do Commander, is capture this hick town called Ch'onan and make it difficult for the North Koreans to move their forces through the road junction. While they're making life difficult at Ch'onan, there will be four or five more landings south of that, designed to convince the North that we are invading in force behind their lines."

"And our men's job is to make it too difficult for the People's Army to move reinforcements south, is that it?"

"Well Commander, no, not quite. The idea is that our men make it difficult but not impossible. We want the North to believe our invasion is for real and that we are trying to stop them reinforcing their army south of us but while they are rushing men and armaments south to repel our invasion, the real invasion will be at Inchon, north or here, hopefully against a much reduced defence."

"Ah. And do we sacrifice our two hundred here to save some thousands elsewhere?"

"No chance Commander. We don't work like that in the US Navy. No, on day four, we go in again and get 'em."

"I like your faith Captain. You mean that I go in again and collect whatever is left!"

"You got it Commander. Any questions?"

"A small suggestion Sir, if I may."

"Sure thing Commander, what's that?"

"Simply that, if you believe in God, that would be a good time to pray."

*　*　*

A young sailor poked his head into the Petty Officer's mess and saw Petty Officer Martin. "Your Captain's waiting to go home, buddy."

"OK, thanks. Thanks for the coffee mate. Hi Ho Hi Ho, its off to work we go."

*   *   *

The two ships steamed in line ahead northwards, keeping well out from the shore to avoid detection. There was little or no fear of detection by North Korean aircraft as the United Nations forces had complete mastery of the air above Korea and over the yellow sea between that country and China. With luck, nobody would know they were there until they chose to show themselves and hopefully, it would then be too late for the Peoples Army to do anything much about it. By nightfall, they were two miles to seaward of their destination, blacked out and silent.

Aboard the Eustace A. Bart, US and British Marines stood by, waiting to climb down the rope scrambling net into the landing craft waiting alongside, engines running. Two Sergeants briefed them quietly. "You know the drill, into the boats and keep silence. If anyone wants a piss, its too late, you'll have to wait until you get back, OK?"

The expected, long suffering laugh at this well worn sally confirmed that everyone was ready for the off. "The American Marine Lieutenant in command nodded to the Sergeants. "OK. Load 'em up."

Challenger stood off, waiting for the landing craft to get away. Once on their way, Challenger would lead them into the creek to provide support if their landing was resisted.

"What's the minimum depth of water in the creek Pilot?"

"At this state of the tide Sir, there should be about four plus fathoms in the centre."

"How wide is the centre?"

"We've got about a mile at most but I wouldn't bet on it Sir. These charts were made by the Japanese just before World War Two and whilst I imagine they kept them up to date when they were in occupation I don't know how careful they were."

"Thank you Pilot. It's always nice to be reassured. OK. Close up Action Stations." In accordance with previous instructions, the ship's company went to Action Stations in silence. The Klaxon alarm was not sounded and there was no shouting, not even any swearing.

Commander Powers lent over the voice pipe beside the binnacle, lifting the weather lid. "Cox'n. Sixty six revolutions. Steer zero eight five. And Cox'n, we'll be making frequent alterations so keep on top line."

" Sixty six Revolutions repeated Sir, course zero eight five. keep on top line, Sir."

Commander Powers smiled to himself; he had just been put in his place by his Cox'n. There had been no need to tell him to keep on top line, Petty Officer Martin was a professional, he'd been in the navy since he was fifteen years old and he didn't need some hard arsed Commander to tell him how to do his job.

The creek into which they were to lead the landing craft was not visible from their present position to the westward of a line of small islands, any one of which could house a gun emplacement but he doubted it. South Korean Intelligence had reported no NKPA activity on these tiny islands and, anyway, they wouldn't be expecting a bloody great destroyer to try and slip between them. There was nothing behind them to interest such a ship, just small inlets, more small islands and, behind a promontory pointing almost due north, the creek leading four miles into the interior but having no military significance. It didn't go anywhere, there was no small port at its head, in fact, no one in their right mind would try to insert a two thousand ton destroyer drawing seventeen feet of water into it. Tailor made for the Royal Navy, Powers thought as he looked ahead through his night glasses.

No lights could be seen either on the islands or on the shore behind them. None of the marines in the landing craft was having a crafty smoke and exposing a red light to be spotted from the shore. The four landing craft chugged at their maximum of ten knots towards the gap just visible between two of the islands.

Powers spoke without taking his eyes off the boats. "They have good crews on those boats Pilot, no wandering about all over the ogin, straight line for the gap. hope there's no one there to receive them."

"Reported uninhabited except for occasional fishermen, Sir. 'Course, you can never be sure that the ROK intelligence is a hundred percent. What do we do if they get shot at?"

"Difficult Pilot. If its only small arms fire, they will ignore it and so shall we. If its anything big enough to do serious damage, they may divert one of the landing craft to go and sort it out but, if its something really big then I suppose we shall have to do something about it. Pity though, don't want to give the game away so soon."

"I suppose it depends upon whether they have radio communication with the mainland, eh Sir?"

"And, how are we supposed to know that, Pilot?"

"Ah. Sorry Sir. Stupid of me."

"Cox'n. Port ten…. Steady…. Steer zero six eight."

"Steer 068. Course 068 Sir."

The gap between the two islands was little more than a quarter of a mile and from the bridge of Challenger, appeared to be a great deal narrower. Looking through his glasses, Powers watched the four landing craft slow to reduce engine noise and, in line ahead, slip through the gap.

"Cox'n. Forty six revolutions."

He heard the bell of the engine room telegraph in the wheelhouse ring to acknowledge the instruction. "Forty six revolutions repeated Sir."

"What's the tide supposed to be like in here Pilot? Any idea? I'm down to six knots with no room to drift if there's a cross current."

139

"The book says we should be alright Sir but I would advise a few more revs as soon as possible."

The last of the landing craft was through the gap and he could see a splash of white water at her stern as she increased speed again, pulling ahead "Cox'n. Sixty six revolutions please."

The order was repeated back and he could feel the ship moving a little faster and a little more positively; even at eight knots, anything approaching a cross current or tide rip could set them on to the mud of one of the islands or even ashore.

Ahead of the landing craft he could see another small island not named on the chart but shown as being right in the centre of the entrance to the creek. The first of the landing craft turned to starboard keeping to the south of the island and steadied on its new course; the others followed it round.

"Cox'n. Starboard twenty.........steady........steer one zero five."

"Steer 105 Sir. Course 105."

Challenger followed the boats round into the creek proper where he felt a little safer. The chart showed him that he had room to manoeuvre and water under his keel. "Cox'n. Down to four six revolutions again please."

The cox'n repeated the order and confirmed it.

"Right Pilot. Now we wait. We just follow slowly up the creek as far as we safely can, trying not to attract too much attention to ourselves but if any attention is attracted, it had better be to us rather than to those little boats, eh?"

"Yes Sir. What do you think?"

"Think? I stopped doing that the moment I agreed to carry out this hair- brained scheme. I should hate to try and get out of here in reverse gear and I really don't much like the idea of trying to turn round but nils desperandum Pilot. We've been lucky so far."

Lieutenant Darling, the navigating officer poked his head

under the forebridge canopy and checked the tell-tale that measured distance travelled over the ground.

"About one more mile's as far as I would recommend Sir."

"OK Pilot."

In the darkness in front of them, the four landing craft were pulling ahead. They were still doing their ten knots compared with Challenger's six. So far, there had been no indication that they had been spotted from the shore. Even the destroyer that must appear huge in the confined creek, appeared to have got away with it. Ahead of them a small blue light flashed to indicate that the landing craft had reached their intended landing site. On the starboard side of the bridge the Yeoman of signals read the message visible only through his binoculars.

"Thank you and good luck, Sir."

"Thank you Yeoman. No reply. Don't want to illuminate half of south Korea with one of the signal lamps, do we!"

"Cox'n. Stop engines."

"Stop engines Sir. Both engines stopped."

"Right. Chas. Ease out the starboard anchor, quietly as you can. I want to swing her round so that we can use our after guns to support the marines if we have to and so that we are pointing in the right direction should we need to evacuate this position in a hurry. I don't want to be fuffing about trying to do a three point turn with North Korean gunners shooting at me."

Lieutenant Turner had been expecting this order and had his foc'sle party standing by in the shelter behind 'A' gun. He handed the bridge over to Lieutenant Darling and ran down the ladder.

"OK Petty Officer?" He addressed the Petty Officer in charge of the Foc'sle party. "Quiet as you can eh?"

The men moved forward and knocked off the Blakes Slip on the anchor chain whilst taking the weight of the chain on the capstan drum. The Petty Officer ME manning the capstan waited for the signal then, on command, let the drum rotate, slowly paying out the chain through the hawse pipe. The hawse pipe had been lined with greased rags ready for this operation and it would have been very bad luck indeed had anything been heard ashore.

Sufficient cable paid out, Commander Powers ordered slow ahead on the port engine, pushing the ship ahead against the cable until he felt it bite and hold the ship.

"Ah well, it should work."

For a moment, the ship appeared to have stopped then, slowly, whilst her bow stayed where it was, upstream of the anchor, the stern began to swing round. If the anchor held, the stern would swing all the way round and the ship would face the other way, ready for a fast getaway if needed. Her after main armament, 'X' and 'Y' guns would be facing the beach on which the marines had just landed and could give supporting fire if required.

On the bridge, Commander Powers watched as the moon rotated round the ship, breathing a sigh of genuine relief when the Pilot announced that the turn had been completed.

"Cox'n. Stop port engine."

"Port engine stopped, Sir."

"On the whole, Pilot. I'd rather not need to do that again. You've got to hand it to those Japs though, the chart appears to be about right as far as depth of water and width of the channel goes, all sorts of things could have changed since they drew them in nineteen thirty eight."

Darling was about to respond when a burst of automatic fire broke the silence.

"Oh dear. Our friends are discovered. Ah well, if they need any help they'll tell us. Now that their presence is no longer a secret, they can use their radio to tell us what they want and where they want it."

Standing under the forebridge canopy, the Yeoman wearing

earphones waited for the marines to report. As they waited, the four now empty LCP's dashed past them in a hurry to remove themselves from any action that might ensue. They would have to take their chances when they came back to lift off the marines in a few days but there was no percentage in getting shot up unnecessarily.

There had been no more gunfire after that one burst and it was generally hoped that that had either been an accidental discharge or a single small engagement. Ashore a sudden flash of light, followed by more gunfire broke the silence and the darkness.

Instinctively, the Yeoman's hand pressed the headphones tighter against his ear whilst with the other hand, writing on the signal pad in front of him. He handed the top sheet of paper to the Captain.

"Local Mayor (or whoever) uncooperative. Sorry about the noise.

"OK for you to go home, no serious opposition encountered. Suggest you retire gracefully and invite the air arm to provide an over flight in the morning just to see what's about."

"Foc'sle. Get it up, quick as you can, you can make all the noise you like now but don't show any lights. Pilot, can you see the island at the entrance to the creek?"

"Not yet Sir but your course is two nine seven."

"Thank you."

"Up and down." The report from the foc'sle could be heard clearly.

"Aweigh."

"Cox'n. Slow ahead both engines. Steer two nine seven."

"Slow ahead both. Steer 297. Course 297, Sir."

"Thank you. Six six revolutions."

The sixty six revolutions were repeated back and the ship

could be felt to be almost surging ahead. On the foc'sle the grey mud covered anchor was secured; it could be hosed down later.

"Clear the foc'sle."

"I can see the island now, Sir."

"Thank you Pilot. Do I go to starboard or to port of it for the deepest water?"

"Keep to port of it Sir. There's a shoal shown to starboard."

The island to starboard, Challenger turned to port and headed for the gap between the islands through which she had come earlier. Under her keel, a now ebbing tide helped her on her way. "If it's all the same to you Sir, I think I'd rather not do that too often."

They were once more at sea, Action Stations had been stood down to Defence Stations and hot cocoa sweet enough to stand the spoon up in was held in almost everybody's hands.

"I rather enjoyed the adrenalin rush myself Pilot. Have you no sense of adventure?"

"No Sir. I'm a navigator not a commando."

"You're old before your time Pilot, that's your trouble. Still, if you insist, I shall refrain from repeating this little adventure until we need to go in and get those poor bastards out again and remember Pilot, by then the enemy will be waiting for us and doing all they can to prevent our little mercy mission."

"Perhaps if we asked them nicely, Sir?"

"I doubt it Pilot but you can try if you wish. I'll put you ashore the day before and you can go and find someone to negotiate with."

"Would you mind awfully if I didn't, Sir?"

"No Darling. I would think you some sort of idiot if you did. Now, breakfast I think."

The First Lieutenant, relieved from his Action Station duties at the damage control centre had come back on to the bridge to see what was going on.

"Ah, there you are Number One. Not much of a do, was it?"

"You know me, Sir. I'm for the quiet life."

"Suddenly I'm surrounded with old women. Ah well, good morning gentlemen. I'm off for something to eat. I suggest that you do the same Number One, while you can.

"Pilot. You had better have your yeoman check the depth recorder record. See if it agrees with the chart, eh?"

"In hand, Sir."

Heading out to sea again, all those on the bridge felt a sense of relief. Above them, the night sky was cloudless and a million stars shone through the blackness. The moon was due to rise in thirty minutes and by then they would be well out of range of any shore-side guns.

SIXTEEN

Lieutenant Owens watched from his scrub bush hide-hole. The fishermen were apparently unaware of his presence on their island and if they didn't know he was there the enemy soldiers, barracked close to their four 100mm guns, didn't know he was there.

There didn't seem to be much contact between the two groups. The fishermen had, earlier that morning, approached the extensive collection of barrack huts and sold the soldiers some fish but that appeared to the extent of their fraternisation. Encouraging, he thought.

Owens' progress amongst the islands uninhabited except for the gun's crews had been unseen and had presented a great deal of useful information, all of which had been radio'd back to Japan. This island, Yangjong-do, was the last and the biggest of those to be surveyed.

On this island, a relatively large village housed the fishermen's families and an equally large barrack housed about a hundred soldiers. A major gun emplacement faced eastwards towards the main channel into Inchon harbour and would have to be eliminated if the troopships were to approach Inchon as intended.

He remained hidden, watching the fishermen and their families going about their everyday routine, waiting to see if, in spite of his efforts at concealment, he had been spotted. Time would tell.

His plan, such as it was, was to do what he could to survey the island's defences and after reporting these, to consider an approach to the village elders in the hope of obtaining some food. Since landing, he had lived on fish he had caught and wild rice from paddies abandoned by order of the Japanese in the mid forties when they cleared all the islands of population.

Since the departure of the Japanese, the Americans and later the South Korean government had encouraged the recolonisation of the islands and the establishment of a viable fishing industry but the invading North Korean army had once more cleared all the islands except this one.

Owens' problem was to discover whether this was because these fishermen supported the North Koreans and were therefore regarded as safe or simply that the fish was needed on the mainland and the fishermen were therefore left to carry on but watched over closely. An immediate problem was, as always when operating close to habitation that a dog, bored with lying in the sun, would come sniffing around and draw someone's attention to his hiding place. Any barking by such a dog would attract the attention of the equally bored children who would come to see what the dog had found.

The day dragged on and no dog found him. He ate what remained of the fish and rice he had managed to boil two days before on an island where his small fire would not be seen and waited for evening. He knew that the boats would go out into the channels to fish with lights during the night, shining lights down into the water to attract fish to the surface. Early in the morning, they would check the nets they had strung across the lesser channels and collect what had swum into their basket traps. It was too dangerous to sleep but he managed to relax and make himself as comfortable as the situation allowed.

What would he be doing now if he were at home? Probably thinking of going down to the local pub. Now there's a thought he thought, better try another way of passing the time; he could actually taste the beer.

*   *   *

Challenger steamed almost due west towards the rendezvous position agreed with the American ship and kept watch over the landing craft that, now that they were far enough off shore, had slowed to their most economical speed to await their mother ship's return. The sun rose behind them, making visual lookout for aircraft difficult but radar would warn them if anything approached from the shore.

"Bridge, Plot. Radar has contact twelve miles, bearing 280. Course and speed of contact, 100 degrees fifteen knots."

As always, the Navigating officer had the morning watch. He glanced in the given direction and, seeing nothing, leaned over the voice pipe. "Thank you Plot. Keep on it. With luck it will be our American friend but don't take anything for granted." He opened the weather lid of the voice pipe to the Captain's sea cabin. "Captain Sir, radar contact two eight zero, twelve miles."

"Thank you Pilot. Our American friend, do you think?"

"Right direction and she's doing fifteen knots so it could well be her. I've told Plot to keep an eye on her and not to assume that she's friendly until we see the whites of their eyes."

"Very wise Pilot."

"Should we go to Action Stations, just in case, Sir?"

"Yes please Pilot. I'll be up in a minute."

Lieutenant Darling hit the red button for the Klaxon. Tired sailors shook themselves awake in the Defence Stations to which they had retired only a few hours before.

"Bridge, Wheelhouse. Cox'n on the wheel Sir. Course two six five degrees, sixty six revolutions showing."

The Pilot acknowledged the report. "Thank you Cox'n."

The telephone behind him whined as someone wound the sound power handle somewhere within the ship. "Morning Pilot. First Lieutenant closed up in the damage control centre. Couldn't you have waited until after breakfast?"

"Sorry Sir. Probably a false alarm but we have a surface contact on radar. Probably the Useless Eustace but thought we'd better close up, just in case."

"Well done Pilot. We'll make a naval officer of you yet."

"Morning Pilot." Commander Powers climbed up the ladder onto the bridge. "Better tell the children to stop and wait until we have identified our visitor."

"Very good Sir. Yeoman. Tell the landing craft to stop. Tell them we have a radar contact which may be their mother but to wait here until we tell them all is in order."

The Aldis lamp mirror clicked up and down as the yeoman pulled the trigger transmitting the message; from the leading landing craft an answering Morse 'R' confirmed that the message had been received and understood.

"Message acknowledged Sir."

"Thank you Yeoman. Pretty morning isn't it?"

"It's a bit too pink for me Sir but that could just be the bloodshot eyes I'm looking through."

"Yes, it was a long night wasn't it. "

Throughout the ship, guns trained and elevated, testing their circuits, ammunition hoists were tested, all ready use ammunition lockers checked to ensure that they were full and, as always, in the galley, the chef made Kye, the thick, sweet cocoa that would substitute for breakfast until Action Stations were stood down.

The loud speaker behind the Captain clicked into life.

"Bridge, Director. Gunnery Officer closed up Sir, all guns correct."

"Thank you Guns. Surface contact bearing two eight zero ten miles."

"Contact two eight zero. The gunnery director behind and above the bridge swung round onto the bearing, swept from side to side a few degrees and settled, locked on to the contact. Director locked on, Sir. Main armament, follow director. Boffors train on surface target bearing green one five."

"A knot or two more for manoeuvring, Sir?"

"Yes please Pilot."

"Wheelhouse, Bridge. One zero eight revolutions please Cox'n."

"One zero eight revolutions repeated Sir." The repeater bell from the engine room could be heard on the bridge.

They felt the increase in speed as the faster turning screws drove the ship forward. Behind them, the wake built up to a wall of white water that would follow them wherever they went; the stern itself settled deeper as the screws bit into the water. There was always something exciting about a destroyer increasing speed, her bow coming up, her stern going down and the rush of wind over her decks becoming more noticeable. Even between the eight knots they had been doing and the now twelve knots, there was a noticeable difference. At thirty knots, it was a bit like riding a skittish racehorse, fun but potentially dangerous.

Under the forebridge canopy, the radio speaker clicked. "Challenger, Challenger, this is Eustace A. Bart. I have you on radar bearing one zero zero. Confirm. Over." Yeoman Houser looked at the Captain.

The Captain held out his hand for the microphone. " I have contact bearing two eight zero. I know who I am but are you sure you do. Over."

"Morning Powers. You don't sound any too cheerful. I thought the night went very well according to your report."

"Morning Sir. The night went very well but all too quickly. We didn't get a great deal of sleep."

"You shouldn't have joined if you can't take a joke Commander."

"I can only hope that those poor bastards I put ashore last night think its funny, Sir."

"Not to worry Commander. You can get your head down this afternoon after we've lifted the LCP's. I understand that your orders are to proceed north to recover a previous beach party and return to this position on Friday afternoon to assist us again. Look forward to that and thanks for your help last night."

"Always a pleasure to assist, Captain. I'll guard your chickens 'til you arrive then push off for some peace and quiet."

"Where's that at?"

"I don't know Sir, but hope springs eternal."

"Don't it just!"

The yeoman took the proffered microphone and hung it on the hook under the canopy.

"Yeoman. You may tell the children that their mother is on her way and that they must be very good because she has had a long and worrying night doing nothing very much whilst we have been playing."

"Bridge, Plot Aircraft bearing zero seven seven, ten miles."

"Oh shit!" The Captain's expletive was broadcast throughout the ship as he had pressed the transmit tit on the tannoy microphone as he lifted it out of its crutch. "Director. Aircraft bearing zero seven seven, ten miles."

The director swung round onto the new bearing, followed by the four 4.5 inch guns. "'A', 'B', 'X' and 'Y' guns, HE

Load Load Load. Aircraft bearing zero seven seven, angle of sight four zero, follow director. Bofors train on bearing."

"Yeoman. Better tell the landing craft to prepare for air attack."

Under the canopy, the radio speaker clicked into life again. "Challenger this is Eustace A. Bart. We have aircraft radar contact behind you, bearing zero nine zero. Over."

Yeoman Houser pressed the transmit tit on the microphone. "This is Challenger. Roger. Out."

"How very kind of them to tell us Sir."

"Yes, Pilot. but they'll be no bloody help from there. Yeoman. Tell the landing craft to gather under my starboard side. I'll turn across the aircraft's course so that all guns will bear and the aircraft won't be able to see the landing craft. We may be lucky. Useless Eustace is only ten miles away. If she winds up her elastic, her guns could be in range in quarter of an hour or so."

"She hasn't got a lot to offer, Sir. One five inch for'ard and a few 40mms scattered about."

"I know that, Pilot and she knows that but, with any luck, the approaching aeroplane driver doesn't and the imminent arrival of reinforcements may dampen his enthusiasm a little. We can only hope so."

The ship's head turned slowly to starboard across the course of the approaching aircraft and the four small landing craft made a run for shelter under her lee. Commander Powers grabbed the microphone for the loud hailer.

"Yeoman. Point that thing at the landing craft will you."

"Landing craft." He called, to attract their attention. "Landing craft snuggle up one behind the other four times against my side. With luck, the aircraft won't be able to see you, let alone shoot at you. Apart from that, there ain't a lot you can do but keep your heads down and pray. Stay close to me whatever I do When the aircraft has passed over us I will expect you to run round to the other side out of harms way. OK?" Four hands waved in acknowledgement.

"I may speed up or slow down to confuse the enemy so stay awake down there." He hung up the microphone.

Through his binoculars, Powers could see that the American ship had increased speed. At her stem, a white water bow wave stood high and wide and, no doubt much to the embarrassment of her captain, a puff of black smoke billowed from her funnel.

"Here come the cavalry Gentlemen, he said. Nice of them to join us, don't you think?"

"All guns, this is Director. All guns, SHOOT!"

The barrage into which the approaching aircraft flew should have caused some damage but apparently did not. From the aircraft, a bomb dropped towards them and cannon fire raked the bridge.

The aircraft passed over the ship and banked tightly to try for the landing craft sheltering behind her but they were already running; two going for'ard round the bow to take shelter on the other side and the other two dropping back to go round the stern. To starboard and some distance away, the bomb exploded uselessly.

"Wheelhouse, Bridge. Four six revolutions."

The reduction in speed had the immediate effect of allowing the forward moving landing craft to swing round the bow out of harms way whilst those dropping astern to move under the ship's port side also took advantage. The aircraft, frustrated, swept low over Challenger taking punishment from the Bofors which could depress that far but rendering the larger 4.5 inch guns unable to fire without endangering the ship from the shrapnel of her own shells.

Once over the ship, the aircraft climbed almost vertically, gaining height, away from the guns below it. Above

Challenger, a puff of black smoke indicated where a shell from the American ship had exploded, not far behind the still climbing aircraft.

"Nice one Pilot," the Captain said admiringly." Not bad at all considering the range."

The aircraft broke left and swung round to make another pass at Challenger, running full tilt into four disintegrating high explosive shells from the ship's main armament. Bits of aircraft flew in all directions and none of them looked like a parachute.

The ship rolled back from the recoil of all four guns firing to port together. Alongside, the landing craft crews ducked instinctively as the ship appeared to be rolling on top of them but she recovered immediately and anyway, the wash from the roll had pushed the landing craft away from her side.

"Good shooting Guns. Damned good shooting. I promise I shall never take the piss again."

"Anything to oblige, Sir."

The radio speaker broke into this repartee. "Sheeeiiiit! Now that's what I call shooting. I'm glad you're on our side."

Commander Powers took the mic. from the Yeoman. "Yours was pretty good too, if I may say so. Nice to have you around, Captain."

"How are the LCP's?"

"Safely under my wing Captain. Not a hair out of place."

"OK Commander, I'll take over command of them now. Be grateful if you'd hang around long enough for us to hoist them inboard before you detach."

"No worries, as our Australian cousins say, Captain. I'll tell them to come to you."

A hearty cheer could be heard coming from the landing craft sheltering under Challenger's port side. The Captain leaned over the side of the bridge holding the loud hailer microphone.

"Nicely done. We must dance together again some time. Your mother is now in charge, you may approach her for hoisting inboard. Good luck. It's been nice working with you."

Four hands waved in acknowledgement and their engines could be heard revving up to maximum speed as they fell off to port, heading for the Eustace A. Bart and home, such as it was.

"Wheelhouse, Bridge. One two eight revolutions please Cox'n."

"One two eight revolutions repeated, Sir."

"Starboard twenty."

The ship's head began to swing.

"Meet her Cox'n. Steady on three two zero."

"Course three two zero, Sir."

Powers turned to the officer of the watch. "Well, it's different! Better than stooging about on patrol, eh?"

"If you say so Sir. Personally, I'd rather be at home with my wife."

SEVENTEEN

North, towards the islands on which they had left Lieutenant Owens but far enough out from shore to render them relatively safe from observation and therefore attack, Challenger cruised. At just sixteen knots, what the far distant Admiralty knew to be her economic cruising speed, the ship seemed to relax, to throw off the tension that had inevitably built up within her. After the excitement of the recent past, the ship's company took full advantage of the make-and-mend declared and relaxed in the sunshine, offering up the sailor's prayer; please God make me brown for leave.

It wasn't that there was going to be any leave and as, strictly speaking, the leave referred to in the prayer was home leave, there was absolutely no prospect of that for some time. Sailors being sailors however, habit won through and they lay, sunbathing on every available flat surface, soaking up the sun's rays, grateful for the opportunity to relax and get some shut eye. With radar closed up and lookouts on the bridge, those on duty kept a benevolent watch over their recumbent shipmates.

To the south, HMS Whitesand Bay was giving assistance in the landing of an even larger group of US and UK Special Forces at Kunsan; exactly where Sergeant cook Thomas, US Marine Corps, had forecast that they would. What he hadn't known when he had made that forecast and indeed bet his money that it was correct was that this was not the main landing. The majority of the force assembled at Camp Xray had by-passed Kunsan and continued northwards under strict radio silence and far enough out to sea to avoid detection by the enemy. His was but a small, private war designed to convince the enemy that it was one of a series of major landings; he was going to have a hard time collecting on his bets.

Inshore of the northward steaming Challenger, Consort stood off the island of Taewha-do, her guns trained on the now quite distant island. She had advised Captain D of the probable landing by troops of the Peoples Army and had been advised in turn to stand off and await the arrival of Opossum who, with her shallower draught, could get in closer after dark and send in a boat to take a look-see.

Opossum also had aboard a small contingent of Royal Marines embarked for just such operations and they were the experts. Consort could, with a clear conscience, allow the other ship to take up the challenge.

As Challenger cruised, happily unaware of her sister ship's problems, Able Seaman Arthur stood once more at the stable door of the Ship's Office, leaning on the counter. "Have you heard anything then?" This was now a regular performance.

"I've already told you Bob. The First Lieutenant has asked for a relief for you and, just as soon as we get notification that he's on his way, I'll tell you and you can write and tell your wife that you're on your way home. What else you tell her to do is entirely up to you of course but, if I was you, I'd make sure she understands your priorities. You could mark the envelope 'BURMA', that should do it."

"Cheeky bastard. It's an idea though. Be Undressed and Ready My Angel, yeah, that should cover it eh?"

"Uncover its more likely."

"Oh very funny mate. Can't you chase it up again?"

"No I fucking can't, now piss off and leave me to get on with something useful."

They heard the Tannoy system switch on. "Hands to tea."

"There you are Bob. You get along to your mess and have a nice soothing cup of tea; ask the Killick of the mess to put some bromide in it, why don't you? Calm you down a bit."

"I don't want calming down. I want sending home to see my wife and my baby. I've been out here long enough, I've served my time, it's my right to go home."

"If you still think you've got rights in this man's navy Bob, you're sillier than I thought; now bugger off."

Consort was not having it all her own way. The NKPA had obviously decided that the capture of Taewha-do was important and overhead, an unequal battle was being fought between a handful of World War Two, piston engined Sea Fury fighters called up from the carrier HMS Ocean, standing well off shore to provide just this kind of support. They faced half a dozen MIG jets provided to the North Korean air force by a supportive USSR.

The pilots performed their ballet for which the rules had not yet been written, indeed, may never be written. The MIGs were undoubtedly faster but the old Sea Furies were more manoeuvrable at the slower speed. In spite of the clear superiority of the Russian aircraft, the navy flyers were holding their own and had even shot down one of the enemy.

On the ground below them, the small South Korean Marine detachment and a few South Korean Special Forces trainees who had been on the island preparing to be inserted on to the mainland behind the enemy's lines, fought off succeeding waves of North Korean soldiers landed from the boats not sunk by Consort. They had radio'd for help and had been promised that help was on its way in the form of both the aircraft already doing what they could above ground and in the form of Royal Marines reinforcements due that night; if they could hold out that long.

A Sea Fury screamed across the island shooting at anything it could see outside the South Korean encampment, followed by a MIG determined to kill it. The navy pilot, knowing the MIG was there threw out the air brakes and kicked the rudder bar to his left, pulling back hard on the stick. The MIG overshot its target and found a jubilant Sea Fury on its tail and lacing its fuselage with heavy calibre bullets.

If just one of them hit a vital bit, the pilot knew, he was lost. These modern jets were fast, heavily armed and built to withstand very high 'G' forces in tight turns and dives but they were helpless if the engine stopped!

They were not designed to glide. If they lost power, the only thing the pilot could do was to bail out and take his chances with whatever was waiting for him down below.

The Korean pilot threw his aircraft into a tight turn, turning away from the following Sea Fury and therein lay his error. Had he dived or climbed, he might just have got away with it but in turning away as he had, he had exposed the side of his machine to the attacking Sea Fury.

He knew, as soon as he had done it, that it had been a mistake, he felt the sudden loss of power as the turbine blades of his single jet engine shattered and disintegrated as the Sea Fury's 20mm shells found a weak point in the engine casing and penetrated into its heart. He was lost; he slid back the canopy of his cockpit and fired the ejector seat rockets, lifting himself clear of his now useless and crashing aircraft.

The Sea Fury banked away, leaving the enemy pilot to find his own solution to the problem of landing in the sea. He might be lucky and be picked up, in which case he would certainly live to fight again but that's the luck of the game. The navy pilot had nothing personal against his enemy, they were two soldiers doing their duty. Let the politicians sort it out if they didn't like it, he was off home to Ocean and to refuel and rearm.

With luck, he'd make it back to the carrier with two or three cupfuls of fuel and half a dozen shells; unless he met another MIG on the way back in which case, who knows? It could just be his unlucky day but if he couldn't take a joke, he shouldn't have joined.

Consort was helpless to assist against the aircraft, they could just as easily hit one of their own as the enemy but, unwilling to stand idly by whilst someone else did the fighting, she fired salvo after salvo of 4.5 inch high explosive shells into the part of the island that appeared to have been taken by the invading NKPA. The South Koreans had, they knew, withdrawn into their redoubt, leaving the rest of the island as a free fire zone. As the sun set, Opossum steamed at her best speed towards the island, bringing with her the Royal Marines who would attempt to retake the island.

First, they would try to relieve the pressure on the South Korean enclave, allowing them to break out to assist in the clearing of the invaders from the rest of the island. God knows, it wasn't a very big island but its position made it strategically important to both side.

Once ashore, the Royal Marines could assess the situation and call down bombardment on to identified targets from both Consort and Opossum; this should even the score a little against the numerically superior enemy forces.

* * *

Once more closed up at Action Stations, Challenger approached the island, from which they hoped to extract Lieutenant Owens; that officer had other things on his mind.

As evening fell, his hide-hole was approached by a woman collecting the long dry washing that she had earlier spread upon the scrub bushes in the sun. The woman knelt down to disentangle a child's dress that appeared to have become caught in the bush.

"Hello. American?"

"No. British." He would like to have told her that he was a Scotsman but reckoned that that might complicate the issue unnecessarily.

"Come. The Elders wish to speak with you. You are quite safe now, the soldiers have shut their gate and are eating their food and drinking beer."

Owens extracted himself from the hidehole beneath the bush and followed the woman towards the village. Dressed as he was and smelling as he did, there was little risk of his being noticed by any North Korean soldier who happened to be looking that way.

The woman led him into the main village hut, a sort of long house used by all the villagers for meetings, weddings, festivals and similar activities. Inside, the lamps were lit and the brightness of the light temporarily blinded him.

An old man stood, waiting for him to approach. The woman pushed him forward, nodding affirmatively, encouraging him to approach the old man. "Hello. You are American?"

"No, British."

"Welcome English. You are safe here, the soldiers have closed their gates for the night, they will not interrupt us. First English, I must ask what you do on our island?"

"I must ask you Sir, if you support the People's Republic of North Korea and the soldiers stationed on your island."

The old man's expression altered not an atom from the blank that it had been from the beginning of this rather stilted interview. "If my village supported the soldiers, you would not have been brought here by my daughter. You were not good at hiding English. She saw you when she was placing her washing this morning. It was not possible for you to be brought here during the day so her washing had to remain on

161

the bush until the evening came; much longer than it would normally have done and possibly attracting the attention of the soldiers but there was no alternative. Now. I ask you again English. Why are you here?"

"I am surveying the soldier's position to report back to my Commander."

"And this Commander you report back to, he is going to invade our island?"

"No, Sir. I do not believe so. I think he hopes that it will not be necessary."

"Then he hopes to send boats into the harbour through the narrow channel?"

"I expect so, Sir."

"Then you had better tell him that the channel is also being mined. All the channels are being mined. I think the soldiers know that your Commander is coming."

The old man's daughter bowed to her father and said something in Korean. The old man half smiled and replied.

"My father agrees that you may sit English. I represented to him that you present a threat to neither his dignity nor his person. Please to sit." She indicated that he should sit where he had been standing, in front of and below the old man.

"Your English is very good Madam. I congratulate you. May I ask how you managed to learn English English rather than American?"

"Before the northerners came, I worked for the British Embassy in Seoul. I found it easier if I mimicked their accent rather than expect them to accept my own."

"Very diplomatic. You did very well."

The old man took up the conversation again. "You have means of talking to your Commander?"

"Yes Sir."

"Then, you will go fishing with my daughter's husband tonight. He will show you where the mines are laid and indicate where they will lay more in the coming days. You must tell your commander that it is too dangerous for your ships to come through the minor channels, they must enter through the main channel to the south."

"But, is that not mined also?"

"Yes but your ships would have more room, maybe they can avoid them there."

"Thank you Sir for your advice, I shall of course pass it to my Commander but I shall be grateful for your son in law showing me where the mines are in the narrow channel also."

"Very well." The old man spoke to his daughter again.

"Come," she said. "You may sit with my husband and discuss tonight's fishing. I shall get you food. When did you last eat?"

"I had a little fish and rice this morning, since then nothing."

"You had better eat first then, before you drink the beer which the soldiers give us for our fish."

EIGHTEEN

The sun had dropped below the western horizon and darkness would be upon them within minutes. Challenger edged as close as she dared to the island. Tongyu-do island marked the outermost entrance to the secondary channel through which it was planned that the bombarding destroyers and the landing craft destined for Red Beach would slip unnoticed past Inchon's defending forces.

No light showed from the island and radar showed that no boats were about. Challenger slowed almost to a halt and lowered her motorboat. "OK Chas. Off you go. Get as near to the island as you can and wait for our friend to find you. Remember, don't show any lights and don't make any noise you can avoid. We don't know whether they have any soldiers on the island and I don't want to lose our only motorboat. We'll be back before dawn." In the boat, Lieutenant Chas.Turner and the boat's crew bore away and set course for the slightly darker mass to the east that was the island.

"Not much of a way to spend a night, eh Sir?" The Leading Seaman on the tiller spoke only just above a whisper.

"It's a very silly way to spend a night but if Lieutenant Owens can manage, I imagine that we can. "

Under the canopy amidships, the stoker manning the engine controls felt in his pocket for his cigarettes, remembered the instruction and pushed them back down. It was going to be a very long night if he couldn't have a fag.

Lieutenant Turner did his best to take a bearing of the two ends of the island and quickly calculated their distance from the shore. He spoke quietly to the Leading Seaman beside him. "A little further, I think Hookey then we can stop and await developments."

"What do you reckon Sir? Will he make it?"

"To be brutally frank, I doubt it. He's been ashore now for seven days and if they haven't caught him by now, then they jolly well deserve to lose the war."

"These Bootneck commandos are pretty hot stuff though Sir. Not a job I'd like."

"Nor I. Right, all of you, keep quiet in the boat. Voices carry for miles over the water. We're looking for a very small blue light from the island, OK?" He couldn't see the nodding heads in the boat but assumed that they understood.

"What if he doesn't show, Sir?"

"Then we come again tomorrow night."

"How many nights do we try for, Sir?"

"Two; just tonight and tomorrow. After that we have to assume that he is either taken prisoner or dead. In that event, we must all hope that he is dead. If he's been captured and he talks, as he will, the enemy will be ready and waiting at Inchon."

"He could have found a bird ashore, Sir."

"There is always that possibility Hookey, but Royal Marine officers are not supposed to let things like that get in the way of duty."

"Not like matelots then Sir?"

The Lieutenant considered it best not to answer that. He lifted his binoculars to his eyes again and scanned the shoreline for a small blue light. Nothing.

* * *

In the sampan with the village Elder's son in law, Owens shone the hissing vapour light down on to the water. Beside him the man spoke quietly pointing to the mines just below the surface and tethered to concrete blocks on the seabed. They were in no danger in the sampan which sat on the water clearing the mines by at least three or four feet but any ship, even the shallow draft landing craft would never make it through this channel. If just one vessel hit a mine, she would block the channel and leave the following ships unable to turn back; a situation not to be thought about.

The man hauled up another fish and noisily told the other boats that he was doing very well and made a joke that Owens didn't understand; it was important that all appeared normal to any watcher on shore.

"We will fish here a little longer then we shall try our luck in the other channel. They hadn't mined that last time I was there and they may not think it is worth it but, with careful navigation and luck, your ships could slip through there."

"What they need is a good pilot, eh?"

The man smiled but said nothing. He called to the nearest boat, loud enough for all to hear that he was bored with such good fishing and was going to try his luck elsewhere. "Bet you I catch more than you do," he called.

He hauled up the stone-in-a-sack anchor and sculled the boat towards the other channel, keeping his light burning so that he could be seen from the shore and therefore could not be doing anything that he shouldn't; and so that Owens could see the extent of the mine field.

Not large but deadly effective. In restricted channels like these, very few mines were required to ensure that any incoming ship would be holed and sunk, blocking the channel to all those behind.

The second channel appeared to be almost too narrow to admit anything much bigger than the sampan but as they approached the entrance the water widened out to form an almost perfect fan shape. A narrow spit of mud separated this new channel from the larger one that continued almost due north before turning east to join the main channel that had been carved out by the outflow from the river to the north.

Owens considered that all of these islands must have been formed by silt brought down from the hinterland by this river over the millennia. There were hundreds of them, interspersed by mud banks, sand banks and some very fast flowing inter-bank tiderips offering deep water channels to those who knew where they were. The channel into which his guide was taking him was one such. He could feel the pressure of the flow against the sampan's blunt bow and was impressed that the man could force the boat against it. The boat's shallow draught, just a few inches, allowed it to skim over the surface of the water without too much drag.

"No mines here, the man said. Flow too fast for them to hold, they would be swept away on the ebb."

"Where does this channel go?"

"It is shaped like a bow and enters the main channel about two miles south of the other one. Your ships would save some distance as well as making a big surprise for the soldiers."

"But they would have to get through the outer minefield to reach here, wouldn't they."

"I think there are no more than twenty mines perhaps before you enter this channel. Could not your marines clear them before your ships get here?"

"You seem to know quite a lot about mines and marines for a fisherman if I may say so and, if its not a rude question, where did you learn your English, from your wife? Its been getting better all evening."

"No. We both learned English at university in Seoul."

"Then, how come you're a fisherman?"

"Because that is what my Government says I must be; to keep an eye on the soldiers. You will permit that I introduce myself? I am Lieutenant Yo Kim Nee, Republic of Korea Marine Special Forces. Temporarily based on this stinking mud bank they call an island."

"And your wife?"

"Camouflage and a great comfort. The village Elder really is her father."

Owens shook the extended hand smiling. "I am very pleased to meet you Sir. I am Lieutenant Bill 'Garry' Owens, Royal Marine Commandos. We are well met, I think. Do you really think you could con a destroyer through this channel in the dark?"

"Perhaps, if we stationed a few sampans with fishing lights at critical points."

"It would certainly surprise the enemy."

* * *

Lieutenant Turner sat in the motorboat, his coat collar turned up to keep out the chill. "Another four hours, Hookey then we can drift out to seaward and wait for Challenger to collect us. I'm starving."

Leading Seaman Booker felt in his pocket and extracted the remains of a bar of milk chocolate; a bar of chocolate from which he had surreptitiously been breaking squares during the night. He handed it to the Lieutenant.

"Have a bit of this, Sir Keeps the wolf from the door as they say."

"Very wise of you Hookey Should have thought of that myself."

"No sign of him then Sir. Wonder if he's alright. Still, there's a few hours of night left yet and there's tomorrow night. There's still a chance I reckon."

"Hope so. Good man."

* * *

Challenger crept back towards the shore, using the last of the night behind her to the west to hide her from the shore. To the east, the first suggestion of grey put the low, dark hump of the island into soft silhouette. Radar had the motorboat fixed and the two vessels approached each other silently and without lights.

"No sign of him then Chas?"

"No Sir. Nothing."

"Ah well, we'll have to do it all again tonight I suppose. Hard luck."

The rising sun threw its first rays across the water, illuminating the bridge. "You'd better get yourself something to eat and get your head down for a few hours. No trouble in the boat, I suppose?"

"No Sir. None. In fact, Leading Seaman Booker even thought to take a bar of chocolate with him to quell the pangs of hunger. I should have thought of that myself."

"Ah well, Chas. We can all learn from the old salts We can't know everything."

"I shall know that tonight Sir!"

"Then the operation has been worthwhile whether we collect young Owens or not eh?"

"Oh, I hope we do Sir."

"So do I Chas. Now bugger off and get some sleep. I suspect that your Leading Seaman Booker has been asleep for half an hour by now. Ever since he took a swig from his illicit bottle of hoarded rum."

"I didn't know he had one Sir."

"Neither do I Chas. but in this navy, it is often for the best if we don't know everything."

"Yes Sir, you're probably right."

Powers turned to the voice pipe. "Wheelhouse, One zero eight revolutions. Steer two five nine degrees."

In the quiet of the early morning, the engine room repeater bell could be heard plainly through the voice pipe. "One zero eight revolutions repeated Sir. Steer two five nine."

The bow swung to port, the Cox'n met the swing and held her. "Course two five nine, Sir."

"We want one nine zero in about an hour, Sir."

"Thank you Pilot. You have the bridge. I'm going down for some breakfast. Stand down Action Stations as soon as you are happy."

"Thank you Sir."

With the captain below, the navigating officer did a full sweep of the horizon with his binoculars. "Plot, Bridge. Anything showing on the magic box?"

In the plot, the cursor on the radar scanner rotated, highlighting the echo of the island now falling behind them and, further away, another island.

"Nothing to report Sir."

"Thank you. Wheelhouse. Cox'n,. pipe Stand Down Action Stations. Hands to Defence Stations."

The pipe could be heard throughout the ship and it was possible to actually feel the reduction in tension amongst the ship's company.

The ship's primary function for the rest of the day was to keep out of sight and out of trouble before returning to Tongyu-do for another attempted lift off of Lieutenant Bill Owens.

Ashore, Lieutenant Owens pressed the transmit tit on his radio. Within minutes, he knew, the admiral would be told, awakened if necessary, that the secondary channel through the islands into the port of Inchon was being mined. The admiral already knew that the main channel, the Flying Fish channel was mined or, if he didn't know that, he should have assumed that it was so.

NINETEEN

It would soon be dark enough to take the sampan out towards where he imagined Challenger would be waiting. Last night, the survey of the minefield and the alternative channel had left him so tired that he spent most of the day sleeping in the village Elder's hut; no one would disturb him there. Now, he needed to get back to the ship to arrange for the assistance he had requested by radio. Two, better still three, divers could, he calculated clear the tethered mines in the approach channel. The problem was what to do with them.

The evening turned to night while he watched the horizon, wondering if he would see Challenger silhouetted against the last rays of the sun. Good man. Commander Powers had resisted the temptation to approach the shore whilst he could still see it. With the sunset behind it the ship would have stood out like a beacon for all ashore to see.

Lieutenant of Marines Yo Kim Nee sat in the boat silently, waiting for Owens to decide that it was time to go. They had left his island with the other fishermen and with the increasing darkness to cover them and burning no lights, he had sculled slowly towards the pick-up point; always keeping an island between his boat and the mainland just in case anyone ashore was looking out to sea. He liked the Englishman, there was no side to him; unlike so many that he had met at the British Embassy in Seoul. Foreign Office Wallahs, well schooled in the British attitude to the natives of the countries to which they were posted.

Owens appeared to be a rational human being if not entirely sane; no entirely sane person would be doing what he was doing but he was clearly a professional and Yo Kim Nee liked working with other professionals, it cut down the risk of failure. Yo Kim Nee had no desire to fail, to be captured or killed. He had a young and beautiful wife and had every intention of surviving into a comfortable old age, surrounded by grandchildren.

"OK friend, off we go. We'll try to get back tonight with the two or three divers and shift those mines. If you can organise a couple or three boats to tow them out, we'll anchor them somewhere harmless; can't allow them to just float away and become a danger to navigation."

The island was lost in the night to the east of them and no light or sound came from seaward. "Hope they remember to come."

Yo Kim Nee took the metal bucket from the bottom of the boat and upturning it, held the rim under the water. He placed his ear against the bottom of the bucket listening. "Small boat is coming. Small motor, not a ship's engines."

"Now there's a useful trick, I must remember that."

"The sound travels better through the water and the small airspace between the water and the bottom of the upturned bucket acts as a magnifying medium. It's a bit like your ear with the bottom of the bucket being the drum."

"Yeah. I know about listening to railway lines to hear if a train is coming but I've never heard of it being done at sea with an upturned bucket. Thanks, I'll make sure my superiors hear of it and pass it on."

"Problem is, Englishman, there's no way of telling the direction from which the sound comes so we just have to sit here until they see your little light. If we try to move we could just as easily be moving away from them."

"Well, we can safely assume that they are coming from the west so I'll point my torch that way and see what happens." They settled as comfortably as they could in the boat, waiting for Challenger's motorboat to find them.

"Blue light bearing zero nine zero Sir, can you see it?"

Lieutenant Turner looked through his binoculars. "Yes, there it is. Good. At least we won't have to spend all night out here tonight, eh!"

Leading Seaman Booker turned the boat towards the tiny light and with his toe, told the stoker on the engine controls to move ahead. "Of we go Stokes. Slowly does it eh! Then we can all go home to bed."

"Better have your guns ready, just in case Booker."

"Yes Sir. Good idea Sir. OK you two, he spoke quietly to the other two members of the boat's crew, make sure your guns are loaded and cocked but for God's sake don't shoot anyone inside the boat, OK?"

"Don't worry Hookey, we quite like you really."

Through the binoculars, even in the almost total darkness of the pre-moon night, Chas.Turner saw the sampan resting quietly on the sea. There appeared to be two men in it. "Can you see the boat Booker?"

"Yes Sir."

"Well, there are two men in it and we're only expecting one. Better be ready in case it all goes nasty."

"Right Sir. What if I shoot our man though?"

"Hard luck, I expect the Admiralty will throw you to the Marines."

"Nice to feel secure, ain't it Sir?"

"OK, here we go. On your toes, all of you."

The boat approached the sampan, nudging alongside just as the first of the moon's light appeared.

"Owens?"

"Yes, Chas?"

"Yes. Good to see you."

"Good. Look, I need the two or three good divers urgently, are they with you?"

"I don't know anything about divers Bill. I'm supposed to pick you up and take you home to mother."

"Shit! I radio'd that I've found a minefield right in the way and that, if they arranged for a couple of your divers to meet me here, we could clear it tonight."

"Sorry Bill. Don't know anything about that I imagine that, by the time Sasebo received your message and sent us one telling us what you wanted, I'd already left the ship."

"I told Sasebo this morning damn it!! Ah well, can't be helped. It will have to be tomorrow night now." He stepped from the sampan into the motorboat, turning to his companion. "I'll be back tomorrow night. Can you meet us? Save taking the noisy motorboat too close in."

"Yes. I'll be here same time tomorrow night, OK?"

"That'll be fine. Thanks. See you then."

* * *

Commander Powers was glad to see Owens back on board Challenger but just as mystified by his reference to divers as Lieutenant Turner had been. "I've had no signal from Sasebo about divers, Bill. Are you sure they got your message?"

"Sure as I can be. I didn't ask for confirmation of receipt but they should have got it. If they didn't get that one, then they didn't get any of them and in that case, I've just wasted eight days and nights being very uncomfortable and dirty."

"There is one other explanation. They may have decided to do a Nelson and pretend they didn't receive that message if they think it's too risky. How many do you need? We have three qualified divers but I'm not sure they know anything about mine clearance."

"Oh I'll tell them what to do if they'll come with me."

"Then we'd better ask them. Can't just detail them off for a job like that I'm afraid; have to call for volunteers. Of course, they'll all volunteer but we have to go through the procedure. Meanwhile, why don't you take a bath and get something to eat. Even if you aren't hungry, you smell awful."

"Thank you Sir, any chance of me having a proper bath in your bathroom? A shower will get rid of the muck but a nice long steep in a hot tub would turn me back into a civilised human being."

"Of course. Tell my Steward to ask some of his friends if they have any bubble bath secreted in their lockers; though I doubt if they'll admit to even knowing what it is."

"Probably best not to Sir. Don't want to get anyone into trouble."

"As you say, Bill. Probably best if we don't know."

"There is a snag though Bill. Probably why Sasebo haven't told me about your need for divers."

"What's that Sir?"

"I'm supposed to be somewhere else by tomorrow night."

"Then, you'd better put us ashore tonight Sir, if you can."

"You go and have your bath and I'll sort out your divers."

"Thanks all the same Sir but, if I'm going ashore again tonight it's best if I don't have a bath. I'll have to make sure the divers get good and muddy and fishy as soon as we get ashore; can't have us all smelling like Europeans if there are any NKPA's about."

"You know best Bill. Anyway go and get yourself fed while I get things organised. How are you going to contact your contact if you land twenty four hours early?"

"Can't Sir. We'll just have to lie low until he arrives tomorrow night."

"Rather you than me, then."

*   *   *

176

The three Able Seamen stood, dressed for diving, by the motorboat's falls. "OK you men. You're quite sure you know what I want done?"

The three men nodded. They weren't wearing their air bottles but they were wearing the rest of their gear and were anxious to get into the boat and sit down.

The boat had been lowered and a ladder let down the side of the ship. "OK lads. Off we go then."

Lieutenant Owens let the men get into the boat then, turning to the CO, saluted and followed them. "OK Hookey," Lieutenant Turner told the Leading Seaman in the boat, "back we go."

The mud smelled terrible and the four men rolled in it until they smelled like the mud. If they were going to have to spend the day holed up on this small island, they didn't want to be noticed if the North Korean army decided to put a patrol ashore for any reason.

They separated into two parties of two some distance apart just in case they were discovered and burrowed out hideholes beneath what little vegetation there was and settled down.

"At least we'll get some shut eye Sir," Owen's partner Able Seaman Brown said, getting his head down and closing his eyes.

"That's more than we'll get tomorrow night. It will take us most of the night to clear those mines and get them re anchored somewhere safe."

"When do we get picked up again Sir?"

"Well, if Challenger isn't here and they don't send someone else, I suspect that we're here until the war's over."

"That'll be nice, Sir. A nice quiet number."

"Only if we win."

"Ah, now why did you have to say that Sir. You've probably spoiled my entire day."

"Sorry about that, Brown."

Lieutenant Owens raised his head just sufficiently to allow him to look round the area in which they were hidden. He couldn't see the other pair even though he knew where they were. Good. Well, there was nothing he could do for the present; he might as well follow the example of Able Seaman Brown and get some sleep. The morning would be time enough to worry about the job ahead of them; not the least of which was working out how to contact Yo Kim Nee tomorrow night. He would be in his sampan waiting to receive the motorboat and he and his divers would be on this island.

Lying there hidden, his mind turned again to the prospect of a pint at his local. He swore and Brown asked him what the problem was.

"The problem is, Brown, that every time I try to get my head down for an hour, I think of my local pub and a pint."

"Then you'd better do what I'd do in them circumstances. Dream that your in your local and drinking your pint. The worse that can happen is that you could wake up before you've finished it."

Owens lowered his head on to his arm, closed his eyes and followed Brown's advice.

TWENTY

Challenger nosed through the narrow channel between the two islands and turned to port; the course, surveyed four days ago, was marked on the chart.

Behind her, the four landing craft kept station on her shrouded stern light, following her closely between the islands, allowing Challenger to pull ahead so that, in the event of gunfire from the shore, they would present an extended target.

With no lights to guide them, Challenger relied on the moonlight to check optically the instructions being fed to the bridge from the radar plot below. It had been decided that, although it would have been more sensible to send the shallow draught and highly manoeuvrable landing craft in ahead of the larger ship, Challenger's ability to return any shore-based gun fire whilst the landing craft surged past and picked up the waiting marines made the present arrangement more attractive.

Of course, if there was any shore-based gunfire, there had been none only a few days ago, then it was highly probable that the marines would not be waiting patiently to be picked up by the landing craft. Rather, they might very well have been wiped out or at least delayed in their return to the appointed beach. It was at moments such as this that Commander Power's naturally up-beat temperament came to the fore and, undeterred, Challenger steamed slowly towards the sharp starboard turn required to enter the creek leading to Ch'onan.

"OK Pilot?"

"So far, so good Sir. Radar seems to be behaving itself and Petty Officer Primrose is unbeatable when it comes to interpreting the image on the screen. So far, he has reported every navigational pointer before it has been seen from the bridge."

"Let's hope he keeps it up, eh?"

"Bridge, Plot. Turn to starboard in three minutes Sir."

"Thank you Plot What does the echo sounder say, Primrose?"

"It conforms the chart markings Sir. We are exactly where we should be at this point."

Powers leaned forward in his chair, opening the weather lid of the voice pipe to the wheelhouse below. "Cox'n. Starboard twenty."

"Twenty degrees of Starboard wheel on, Sir."

Powers watched the tell-tale giro repeater under the forebridge canopy tick round as the ship's head swung. "Meet her Cox'n. Steer one two zero."

"Steer one two zero Sir."

The ships head slowed and stopped swinging as the Cox'n turned the wheel the other way, stopping the turn, he met her and returned the wheel to the neutral position, steadied the head on the course ordered.

"Course one two zero Sir."

"Right Yeoman. Tell the boats to go on ahead now and wish them luck."

Behind the armoured shield of 'A' gun, Able Seaman Arthur offered up a short prayer. "Please God don't let there be anyone ashore shooting at us. There's no way we can turn round in a hurry in this bloody creek."

"Amen to that." The Gun Captain, Leading Seaman Archer responded, making sure that the microphone connecting him to the gunnery control Director above him was switched off.

From his position sitting on the hard seat on the right hand side of the gun, his feet on the pedals which would power up the gun's turning mechanism if the power failed, Able seaman Arthur sang quietly to himself, he often did when he was nervous. "Roll on the Rodney, Repulse and Renown, this one funnelled bastard is getting me down."

"Keep silence in the Gun!"

The Gun Captain had switched on his microphone so that he could respond to the Director's instructions but with luck, the Gunnery Officer in the Director had not recognised the voice and wouldn't know which gun was having a sing-along. He tapped the forward-looking gun layer on his head to attract his attention. "Shut up you silly bugger."

To seaward, the USS Eustace A. Bart waited, silent and blacked out, hoping not to hear or see the muzzle flashes from gunfire from behind the row of islands which were screening her from any spotters the NKPA might have and behind which, Challenger and the Bart's four landing craft had disappeared.

"Stop engines. Let go the anchor."

Using the same silent or near silent routine as last time, Challenger drifted up to her anchor, turned and waited. The rearmost 'X' and 'Y' guns now bore and, in 'A' and 'B' guns, the crews relaxed just a little.

"Of course, Sir, the nasties could have let us come on in and will open fire from seaward of us when we try to get out again. If they can bottle us up in here, they could get five for the price of one, as you might say."

"Thank you Pilot. It's always nice to have a happy soul in company when things are a bit fraught."

"Sorry Sir, Didn't mean to put the mockers on anything. Just thought that, if I were organising the opposition, I might try to bag the lot, boats and all."

"Pilot."

"Sir?"

"Shut up."

"Sir."

"How long have we been here?"

"Half an hour, Sir."

"Then it's about time something happened. I don't like it when nothing happens when we should be either hearing or seeing something happening."

"Yes, Sir."

"Plot, Bridge. Anything?"

"Nothing moving Sir.

"Messenger. Pop down and see if you can persuade the galley to give us some Kye. Get some for everybody."

The bridge messenger disappeared down the ladder towards the galley; with luck he would have time for a surreptitious smoke while he was waiting.

"Bridge, Plot. The landing craft are on the move."

"Thank God for that. We'll let them pass us then get ourselves out of here. This is not something I would like to make a career of, however ungrammatical that statement may appear."

"I think it's alright just so long as you don't actually write it down, Sir."

"Thank you Pilot. That's a little better than your last remark, even if it is nonsense."

They waited in silence as the four landing craft passed them. "Looks like they're all there Sir. Can't tell, of course, but the boats seem to be pretty full."

"Thank you Yeoman." Commander Powers lifted the telephone handset and spoke to the focs'le. "Get the anchor up Chas. Quick as you can."

Silence not now being the primary consideration, they heard the reports on the focs'le. "Up and Down, Sir. Anchor's clear Sir."

The telephone rang on the bridge. "Anchor's aweigh, Sir."

"Thank you Chas. Secure for sea. Right, Pilot. Fall in astern of the landing craft and follow them out."

"Wheelhouse. Eight six revolutions. Steer two nine five."

"Eight six revolutions repeated Sir. Course two nine five."

A silent but no less heartfelt sigh of relief encompassed the ship as she gathered way and moved towards the islands and the open sea. All sailors have an inbred fear of being close in-shore, they just naturally like to know that there is plenty of water both under them and on either side.

Ahead of them, a burst of automatic gunfire broke the silence, the muzzle flashes momentarily illuminating the marines in the leading landing craft. "Plot, Bridge. Can you see what they're shooting at ahead of us? Anything on the radar? Is there another ship coming in?"

"Nothing on radar Sir."

"Then it must be the island at the entrance to the creek. They must have seen something on the island."

"Don't see any return fire, Sir."

"That's true Pilot. Neither do I. Now I wonder what's up."

There was no more shooting and as the landing craft passed the island, they turned to port towards the outer islands and the sea.

* * *

The Useless Eustace was waiting. She had not heard the shooting but had seen the muzzle flashes reflected in the night sky behind the islands. On the bridge Captain Cy. Masters swore. He didn't like it when his boats were under fire and there was nothing he could do about it. He couldn't even see them. He waited, hoping to see the flashes from the bigger guns in Challenger taking revenge for any attack upon his marines.

Nothing. Absolutely nothing. "What do you reckon?"

The Executive Officer, standing beside him shrugged his shoulders in the darkness. "Accidental fire?"

"Marines aren't supposed to fire accidentally, Bob."

"We'll be in range of their walkie talkie in a few minutes. We can ask them?"

"If it was accidental and there's any casualties as a result, I want the hide of whoever fired. I want him off this ship and into whatever hell you can find for him as soon as we get back to Japan. Is that clear?"

"Sir."

"I think I can see something Sir."

The Port lookout spoke no more loudly than he needed to to make his report. "Looks like a bow wave, white water or something. Red two five, Sir."

Four pairs of night glasses trained on the bearing. "Yes. There's something there." Captain Masters picked up the microphone from its crutch. "Radar? What do you have on red two five?"

"Can't see anything Sir. Too much ground clutter up against the shore, Sir."

"Well we can see something, try to sort something out will you."

"It's them, Sir." The Exec could see them now. "Four bow waves. Where the hell is the destroyer?"

"Bridge this is Radar. I have one large echo on the bearing requested Sir. There's a lot of snow round it, could be our boats."

"Thank you Radar. Keep on it."

"You all ready to lift the boats Bob?"

"All in hand, Sir. The medics are down there waiting just in case too."

"Good. Hope they won't have too much to do, eh?"

"I'll vote for that, Sir."

* * *

The sun rising in the east was unobscured by any sign of land. The Eustace A. Bart, with all her landing craft inboard and Challenger astern were well to the west of their night's adventure position.

"Challenger, this is Eustace A. Bart. My Captain would like to speak with yours. Over."

The radio speaker on the starboard side of Challenger's bridge crackled into life.

"This is Challenger. Wait. Out."

The Leading Signalman on watch looked at the Navigating Officer who, as always, had the morning watch. He lifted the weather lid of the voice pipe to the captain's sea cabin. "Captain Sir."

There was a pause of only a moment. "Yes? What is it Pilot?"

"Eustace's Captain on the blower Sir. Wants a word."

"I'll be right up. What's it like up there?"

"Lovely morning Sir. Sunrise was as pretty as a picture."

"I suppose I shouldn't have asked."

"Good morning Captain. What can I do for you?"

In the USS Eustace A. Bart, Captain Masters put down the bacon sandwich he had in his hand and picked up the microphone. "Morning Commander. Nice job you did last night. My people tell me you behaved like a gentleman; led them in and followed them out. Thanks."

"All part of the service, Sir. Can you tell me how they did? There didn't look as if there were too many casualties but it was difficult to see in the dark."

"They done good, as far as I can make out. Caused all sorts of mayhem amongst the NKPA units trying to pass down the highway. Took only two fatalities, had to bury them there worse luck but it wouldn't have been practical to try and carry them out. Five serious but walking wounded and fifteen who look as if they have been in some sort of fire-fight but won. The rest are AOK thank God. They made contact with locals who helped them and will maintain some small scale attacks on passing transports. They know enough to let most of the NKPA's reinforcements move south to where we want them. I guess you had no trouble getting in and out?"

"No. Except for a small matter of someone in one of the landing craft trying to shoot his way out all on his own. Must have been heard miles away. Do you know what that was all about?"

"Accidental fire, Commander. Let's just say that one of the guys was a little over excited. He won't be with his unit for much longer. One of the walking wounded got himself in the way of that guy's burst of fire. Not too serious but the medic tells me he's what you Limeys would call a mite upset at being shot by his own side. "

"That's understandable. Glad there wasn't too much damage. If you have no more need of me, I have orders to return north."

"OK. Thank you and God's speed. If we're ever in the same place at the same time Commander, we must go ashore and have a drink together."

"I'll look forward to that Captain. Out. Right Pilot. Course for Inchon?"

"Three five zero Sir. Alter course late this afternoon."

"Very well. Revs for twenty five knots Course as stated. I'm off for some breakfast."

"Wheelhouse, Bridge. Starboard ten."

The giro repeater ticked round, watched by the quartermaster on the wheel and the officer of the watch on the bridge. "Meet her, Quartermaster. Steer three five zero. Two one six revolutions."

The bridge heard the revs being repeated by the engine room repeater and relaxed as, free from company again, Challenger headed north; happy to be on her own again.

In his cabin, David Powers added another page to his letter.

* * *

"Eight o-clock Pilot. You are relieved." The First Lieutenant stood beside the Navigator. "All is in order?"

"All is as it should be Sir. We have parted from our local friendly Yank who has gone I know not where and we are going north again, back to Inchon, at two one six revs. Captain is at breakfast and I shall be in about three minutes if that's alright with you."

"Yes, carry on, I have the watch. Inchon, you say? I wonder why we're going back there."

"No idea Sir. Captain's orders."

"Then to Inchon we must go, eh?"

"Exactly Sir."

"OK bugger off."

The other watchkeepers had also been relieved and the bridge settled down once more.

* * *

In Sasebo, Daphne Archer made her way to the cabin she shared with her friend Roberta.

The flight back from Tokyo had been cold and uncomfortable; Dakota's were excellent working aircraft but the military version of the DC3 was not equipped for comfort.

Her visit to Tokyo, in company with Lieutenant Bowden, had been exciting. Whilst he had been with Admiral Joy, ensuring that Owens' intelligence was transferred to the US navy's charts, she had hit the shops and done considerable damage to her meagre savings but she didn't care.

Once free from Admiral Joy, Terry Bowden had ceased behaving like a Lieutenant RN and had made quite a good fist of wooing her.

Dinner first, they had gone Japanese just for the excitement of something different, then by taxi back to their hotel. Their rooms were on the same floor though not adjoining and Terry had escorted her to her door as a gentleman should. It was at that point that Daphne had decided that, if she didn't determine the programme, nothing more was going to happen.

She opened the door and, as he tentatively leant forward in the hope of a goodnight kiss, she moved backwards into the room, dragging him with her.

She would never admit to her cabin mate that her efforts had been rewarded. What she couldn't wait to tell Roberta, was that she, Second Officer Daphne Archer, was engaged to be married to Lieutenant Terrance Bowden Flag Lieutenant to Admiral Dickenson. Roberta would be as jealous as anything.

Lieutenant Bowden was in Admiral Dickinson's office. "I'm pleased to see you my boy. The big bad American didn't have you hanged, drawn and quartered, then?"

"No, Sir. Admiral Joy suggested that it would be best if you didn't mention this operation to MacArthur. Said that, if you didn't, he wouldn't and that way, he reckons you both may survive the war."

"Sounds like good advice to me. I think we deserve a drink, don't you?"

"There's just one other thing, Sir. Whilst in Tokyo, I asked Daphne to marry me."

"Did you indeed. And what did the fair Daphne say?"

"Yes Sir."

"Do you mean that she said Yes Sir or that she said yes, she would marry you?"

"Yes, Sir."

"Clearly this conversation is going nowhere Terrance, get the drinks poured out; we can celebrate both operations successfully completed, eh?"

"I'll drink to that, Sir."

Admiral Dickenson sipped his drink and thought he had better write to the boy's mother. Daphne was an entirely suitable young woman as well as being quite a looker. She would make the boy a good wife; keep him up to speed. He wished he was at home and could tell her personally; he missed her terribly but could never tell the boy that.

TWENTY-ONE

Lieutenant Owens and the three divers had spent the day keeping an eye out for intruders and trying their hands at fishing for their dinner. This they had done by swimming out from the mud beach and, standing on the bottom, dangling a short line with bait from an outstretched arm and waiting for the fish to come to them. Though not, they decided, a method suitable for commercial exploitation, they had by lunchtime caught enough to feed them.

The wind, such as it was, was from the land and the tiny amount of smoke from the cooking fire blew out to sea where it would not be seen. No super-efficient nose would pick up the smell of boiling fish from that.

"OK, you lot. How much diving experience have you had?"

"We're all qualified divers Sir."

"That's not quite what I mean. What I want to know is do you think you can lift the weighted block holding the mine in position, carry it up to the surface so that it can be lifted into a boat?"

"Don't need to lift it Sir. If the guy in the boat lets out a line, we can attach that to the weight and the guy in the boat can do the lifting. How deep is it where we'll be working Sir?"

"Not more than about forty feet, I should think. Could be less in places. Is that a problem?"

"No Sir. That's OK. How much do you reckon these weights weigh?"

"Presumably only just enough to hold the mine in position. I don't suppose they wanted to carry about any more weight than they needed to when laying the mines. Say about fifty pounds? Something like that I should think."

"Then we shan't need heavy line for the job. Something about half inch should do it; what do you think Alf?"

Able Seaman Alf Barnett agreed that that should be sufficient but a little heavier would be better, just in case.

"Right. We'll just have to hope that the sampans carry the kind of rope we need. Can't contact them before they get here tonight."

"Why don't we just cut their mooring and tow them out to sea, Sir?"

"Can't do that. They'll float about all over the place and some poor sod will steam into one or more of them. The nasties have already set free lots of floaters and two of the Yankee destroyers have blown their bows off by hitting them."

"What if we just pull them down to their weights and tie them off just about a foot or two from there. That way, they will be too deep for any of our ships to hit them and we don't have to spend a lot of time towing and anchoring them somewhere else?"

"Brilliant in concept Brown but what if they can be set off by the movement of the water around them? A destroyer, going at say ten knots would set up quite a serious disturbance around its screws. If the mines are too near the bottom, one could be pushed against either the bottom or even its own weight and explode; it would only take one to hole a ship and block the channel."

"S'pose so Sir. Just an idea."

"It's probably a very good idea but this isn't the time to test it. Too much depends upon our ships getting through the channel and into position to bombard the shoreline. The landing craft will be depending upon the ship's big guns to knock out anything the nasties have ashore."

"Well, we can spend some time this afternoon testing our kit, that will give us something to do. I hate sitting about with nothing to do, Sir. Not in my nature, as you might say."

"Good idea. Right. Bury your food rubbish and then you can get on with checking everything. I'm going to sneak about a bit."

Owens crawled away from their bivouac in search of a suitable depression into which he could slide and relieve himself unseen; the divers had managed to relieve themselves under water earlier and he had not asked them how they had accomplished it.

As always, when you were in a hurry for the night to come, it took forever. Owens remembered, as a child, wanting Christmas Eve to pass so that Santa Clause could come down the fire-less chimney into his bedroom and fill the stocking that his mother had drawing-pinned to the mantelpiece. That one evening had seemed like a whole extra twelve months.

Challenger steamed northwards, well out from any possible observation from the shore.

"Alter course in one hour Sir. New course will be zero nine zero. Should be in position by ten o-clock."

"Thank you Pilot."

Commander Powers sat in his sea chair, relaxed and happy. He didn't know if Owens would be waiting for them but they had agreed that, if possible, Challenger would return to pick him up, together with his three divers but no date had been set for this, only an agreement that if Challenger returned, his boat would be waiting off-shore at four in the morning. Any later and they risked the sunrise before they were clear of the area and any earlier, Owens might not have finished mine clearing.

It was all a bit airy-fairy but it was the best they could do. There was nothing in Powers' orders about going back if Owens missed the scheduled rendezvous as he had. The ship was not to be hazarded playing cowboys and indians off Inchon and anyway, it could jeopardise the whole operation if she was observed standing off and on night after night. He hadn't told Sasebo what he was doing and, if they didn't ask, he wouldn't.

* * *

Lieutenant Yo Kim Nee sculled his sampan in towards the beach where, he had seen Owens' blue light; must have arrived early. He could see nothing ashore but then, he didn't expect to do so. Owens was too much of a soldier to show any light until he knew who might see it. Ashore, four pairs of eyes watched the boat coming towards them.

"What do you reckon Sir?"

"There's only one man in the boat so I hope it's our man. If it ain't, he's gong to be very dead very quickly."

"We haven't got any weapons Sir."

"Yes you have. You have your knives and your hands. If you can't kill someone with either or both of them, you've no business being in this business."

"But we ain't Sir. We're either Able Seamen or Divers. We ain't commandos like you Sir."

"Then now's your chance to learn Brown. Now shut up and let's see what he does."

Yo Kim Nee ran the sampan onto the muddy beach and sat, quietly waiting to see what happened. If he was right, the Englishman would appear and they could get to work. If he was wrong, he had either wasted his effort sculling the boat this far or worse, if the Englishman had been captured and talked, he was about to be shot.

The shadow on shore moved. Had he not been watching for just such a movement he wouldn't have seen it but now he could see the silhouette of a man against the stars behind him.

"Nice of you to come."

"Owens?"

"Yes. I have three divers with me and we've been holed up here all day so we're more than ready to get to work."

Three more shadows materialised beside the man on the beach. "OK you lot, into the boat and quietly does it."

They pushed the boat off the mud and climbed into it, lifting their kit in first. The Korean looked at them. "Do you know what you have to do?"

"No problem mate. Just you show us the mines and we'll shift 'em."

Yo Kim Nee smiled; typical of the English sailor. No respect for the natives but in war, your enemy's enemy is your friend; he would not tell them that he was an officer in the ROK Marines.

"Let me introduce you. Lieutenant Yo Kim Nee of the Republic of Korea Marine Corps, these three are Able Seamen from Challenger and what is much more important tonight, they are experienced divers."

An embarrassed silence followed this announcement but was soon broken by Able Seaman Brown. "We shall need some lengths of one inch line to lift the mine's anchor blocks into the boat Sir. Have you anything like that?"

The use of the title Sir allowed the Korean to forget the earlier lack of respect and he nodded in the darkness. "Yes, no problem. I have six boats and all of them will have the rope you require, what do you propose doing?"

Owens explained the idea of lifting the weights off the bottom and then towing both the mine and the weight out of the channel and into a safe position. There, the weight would be released to take the mine back down, out of harm's way.

194

"I like it. If your men can loop the end of the rope through the ring on the weight, the man in the boat can haul it off the bottom and make it fast to the thwart then tow the mine out of the channel. Once clear, he has only to let go the line and the weight will sink back down to the bottom, taking the mine with it." He sculled the sampan expertly back towards the main island and the channel where five other sampans with trusted fishermen waited, fishing.

* * *

Challenger lay, stopped to seaward of the biggest of the off-shore islands in the hope that, if the NKPA had any radar on shore, the ship would be shielded by the island.

"How long, Pilot?"

"About another hour, I should think Sir."

"I daren't move about out here in case our movement attracts attention. I reckon we're safer sitting still than moving about. Number One, you did make sure that the boat's crew was fed before they went off and made sure they knew that they have to wait as long as possible but not after four thirty?"

"All covered Sir."

"I didn't doubt it Harry, just talking it through for my own benefit. Hate to cock up something simple."

* * *

Able seaman Brown looped the one inch manila rope through the ring on top of the last mine in his area. He had seen ten lifted and taken away be a succession of sampans. Where they were taking them he didn't know and, frankly, didn't care. He was cold and tired and wanted out. He gave the agreed two tugs on the rope and watched as the weight lifted above him and slowly drifted sideways away from him towards the sea as the boatman sculled his craft away.

He looked about him. He couldn't see any more mines but then, he hadn't been able to see any of them until the boatman had shone his bright fishing light down into the water. For all he knew, there might be hundreds of the blighters and he was tired and needed a rest. Another boat appeared above him, shining its light down into the water. Slowly it moved to the right then the left, zig zagging up the channel, looking for more mines. He looked at his air supply gauge. Not bad. He still had about a quarter of an hour's air left.

The light found no more mines, the gauge said five more minutes and that was too small a safety margin. He pushed himself up to the surface and looked about him.

The boat was immediately to his left and he reached out for the gunwale. Hands grabbed his and helped him into the boat where he pulled off his facemask. "Shit! I don't want to do that too often."

The fisherman looked at him and smiled but said nothing. He took up his scull again and made towards the other boats gathered at the seaward end of the channel.

"OK Brown?"

Lieutenant Owens helped him transfer into the other boat and waved a thank you to the fisherman who sculled away quickly, leaving them in the dark.

Yo Kim Nee came alongside in another sampan and took them both inboard. "OK English? You want to go home now?"

"You have no idea!"

"I can imagine. Not what you might call a pleasant way to spend an evening, eh?" With the divers resting in the bottom of the boat, Yo Kim Nee sculled slowly towards the outer island and the sea.

* * *

Leading Seaman Geof Booker saw them first. "Boat coming Sir."

It was ten past four in the morning and they had been sitting there, waiting since midnight.

"Got them, thank you Booker." Lieutenant Chas Turner was as relieved as Booker that their vigil might soon be over.

"Stand by in the boat. "

He heard the three men of the boat's crew cocking their Lanchester automatic rifles; he hoped that they wouldn't need to use them.

"Boat ahoy."

"Challenger."

"Thank God for that. Is that you Owens?"

"Yes, and your divers. We're all buggered but we've cleared the narrow channel."

"Great stuff. Come aboard. We were just about to give up on you again. My instructions were to wait until four thirty and then get the hell out of here."

"What time is it?"

"Four -twenty!"

"Then you've all sorts of time left. There's no hurry."

Yo Kim Nee shook hands with all four men and invited them to take a beer with him when they had won the war.

"My respects to your wife and to her father Sir. I'd be obliged if you would tell him that I appreciate all the help he gave me."

"If what you are planning is successful English, you can thank him yourself soon."

"I shall look forward to that Sir. Goodbye and thank you. Right Chas., home we go eh?"

The motorboat stood out to sea and the sampan sculled slowly towards the shore. It was exactly half past four.

TWENTY-TWO

One of the much cherished advantages of a detached command is that, at any given moment, nobody is absolutely sure where you are or what you are doing; thus it was that Commander Powers had been prepared to dash back north in the hope of collecting Lieutenant Owens and his divers. With these men once more onboard, Challenger wound up to maximum speed and drove south towards Kunsan.

As September twelfth was his birthday Powers was determined to enjoy it. At thirty two knots, the ship was not at its most comfortable but the exhilaration added something to his general feeling of satisfaction and good will to all men.

At this speed, they would be off Kunsan by early evening and only then would he know what the score was. Whitesand Bay had assisted in the landing of more than a thousand US and British marines five days ago and, as far as he knew, all was going according to plan. The plan being, of course, to convince the North Korean's that this was the expected invasion and the frigate's duty had been to get in close and give short-range assistance to the landing troops.

Further out to sea, the Americans had stationed a couple of cruisers for longer-range bombardment and an aircraft carrier to provide air cover for the marines as they fought their way inland. Challenger's job, as he understood it, was to assist by adding her fire power to the general bombardment.

The initial landing had been covered by the rocket ships blanketing the beach ahead of the advancing landing craft and, subsequently, providing a rolling barrage ahead of the marines as they landed but these would by now have retired as the war progressed too far inland for them to be of any assistance.

With the Frigate's four inch guns taking out notified targets within five miles of the coast and Challenger's larger four point fives taking out such targets at up to eight miles, the American cruisers with their nine inch guns could, even from three miles out to sea, lay down a devastating barrage at up to twelve miles inland. This would be a good day to be at sea, rather than on shore at the receiving end of this combined firepower. With the night-time bombardment including Star Shell to illuminate the battlefield, the effect, he thought, would be much the same as a firework display; quite a way to celebrate his birthday.

He turned as the yeoman knocked on the doorpost, signal pad in hand. "Seems we aren't required after all, Sir."

He read the signal and handed the pad back to the yeoman. "Thank you Yeoman." He spun the handle on the sound-power telephone above his desk, putting the handset to his ear.

"Bridge? It seems we are surplus to requirements after all so there's no need to blow her boilers; come down to one two eight revolutions. Ask Pilot to come and see me, will you. Course three five five."

His instructions acknowledged, he returned to the charts spread out on the table in the centre of the cabin. "Ah well, there goes my firework display!"

Lieutenant Darling knocked on the doorpost of the curtained doorway. "You wanted me Sir?"

"Ah, Pilot. Yes. It seems that Kunsan can manage without us, I imagine Whitesand Bay will be pleased not to have to share her thunder with us. We, it seems are requested and required to proceed once more into the breach up north."

"Is this it then Sir? The real one?"

"Very probably Pilot. It seems that Cossack and the others are already there and we are to join by 0800 tomorrow. I've come down to economical cruising speed and I'll leave it to you to give the Officer of the Watch a course and speed to rendezvous in the position given." He handed the Navigating Officer the signal.

"What will they want us do Sir?"

"I've no idea but I imagine Captain D is a bit miffed by our being detached for so long and escaping the boredom of the patrol so, I expect he will find us something nice to do; something uncomfortable I expect."

*   *   *

Attending upon Captain D in Cossack, Commander Powers had to admit he had never seen anything quite like the armada spread out around them. "How many ships are there here, Sir?"

"Now that you've been good enough to join us David, two hundred and sixty one. I did assure the Supreme Commander that we could probably manage without you but he insisted. Seems you've done something to impress him. I'd be grateful if in future you'd restrain your natural ebullience when dealing with these Americans, particularly soldiers; we are, you will remember, supposed to be the silent service."

"Yes Sir. You don't mean Big Mac himself, do you Sir?"

"Certainly I do. He instructed me to congratulate you but as he didn't tell me why, I shall do no such thing. Perhaps you could enlighten me?"

"No idea Sir."

"Very well. We'll forget the whole thing. Now. I understand that we are to proceed through this narrow channel, he pointed to the chart on the table in front of them, and take up station at intervals from north to south in the main channel north of Inchon harbour itself. We are to provide covering fire for the landing craft going in to Red Beach." Again he pointed to the chart.

"I understand that the usual channel round to the north of the harbour is mined but that this narrow channel here is clear. I can't imagine why, if they took the trouble to mine the proper channel they wouldn't ensure that there wasn't a usable alternative but there you are. I intend to proceed with great care, I can assure you."

"That channel is clear Sir."

"And how do you know that David?"

"My divers cleared it two nights ago, Sir. We had the assistance of the local fishermen led by a Lieutenant Yo Kim Nee of the ROK Marines and the help of our own, semi-tame Royal Marine Commando, Lieutenant Owens."

"I see. So that's what you've been up to. Some fellows get all the fun."

"I took the liberty Sir, of arranging with the local fishermen to light the channel for us, if we tell them when we will be coming through. I could send Lieutenant Owens back ashore to set it up, if you wish."

"Are they reliable, these locals?"

"It seems they saved Owens life and helped our divers clear the channel by shining their fishing lights down into the water to illuminate the mines. Our divers then attached a line to each mine and the locals calmly towed the damned things away and dropped them somewhere else."

"Did they now? Now that's quite a thing to do, don't you think?"

"To be perfectly honest Sir, I'm damned proud to have been associated with the operation but Owens has to take the credit. His job was simply to creep from off-shore island to off-shore island, locating and reporting the positions of the North Korean gun emplacements defending the port but the fishermen told him about the mines. It was his idea to go back and clear them."

"How long was he ashore then?"

"Ten days, Sir then another to clear the mines and wait for us to pick him up."

"When this little lot is over David, I'd like to meet your Lieutenant Owens.   He sounds like a good man."

"For a Royal Sir, he's almost civilised."

"And, David, when you finally leave the Service, you'd better try the diplomatic lot, sounds like you might be quite good at it.

"OK. I've asked the other Captains to join me for lunch and a briefing. It might be better if you do that but I insist on leading my Flotilla through the channel, I'm damned if I'm going to be upstaged by you. Mind you, if I hit a mine, you had better be somewhere else when this party is over. Somewhere very far away."

"Sounds reasonable Sir. Thank you. With your permission Sir, I'll instruct Lieutenant Owens to go ashore and organise things?"

"Yes David, do that. We'll all get ourselves organised over lunch."

*   *   *

The captains gathered in Cossack's wardroom, the only space big enough in the destroyer. The dining table, which could nominally sit sixteen, was covered with charts; the relevant channels and navigationally important islands and mud banks marked in different colours by the Navigator's Yeoman who had had something to say about doing colouring-in at his age.

"Welcome Gentlemen." Captain D had waited until all were present. "Thanks, it seems that due, to some totally unfair detached duties by David here," he nodded at David Powers, " those of us who have been trundling up and down this coast week after boring week, are now to be invited to what will, it is hoped, be the NKPA's going away party.

"On the table, Gentlemen, you will have observed a set of charts of which there will be a copy for each of you when you leave here. On these charts you will notice that we shall not be entering Inchon in the normal manner but via an, until now, un-surveyed channel. That, amongst other things such as mine clearing, landing landing parties and generally swanning about, is what David has been doing since he left us."

An unidentified voice mumbled something about lucky buggers getting all the fun but D ignored this.

"It seems that, just to ensure that your navigation is not likely to put any of you ashore or likely to block the channel to those behind you, David's new friend, Royal Marine, Lieutenant Owens, is, as we speak, arranging with the local fishermen to light the channel and lead us through. They, will give the impression that they are fishing as normal at various points along the channel and their headman's son in law, who turns out to be a Lieutenant in the ROK marines, will lead the first ship through. Needless to say, Gentlemen, Cossack shall be that first ship."

Coffee and sandwiches were served as the assembled officers studied the charts on the table.

*   *   *

With over two hundred ships assembled off-shore, there was little point in trying to be secretive about his approach to the island but Owens was unwilling to get himself shot at at this stage of the operation. Challenger's motorboat dropped him off the beach as far from the military installation as possible and without even slowing down.

If observed, as it should have been, the boat would have been assumed to have been reconnoitring a possible landing position; Owens would not have been seen rolling over the seaward side into the water and staying down for as long as he could so that any watcher's eyes, watching the boat, would have moved on before his head broke the surface briefly before once more submerging as he swum towards the beach.

If there was an NKPS sentry standing there waiting for him, it would be unfortunate but he suspected that most of them would be inside their gun emplacement, waiting for the ships to make an attempt at entering Inchon at the next high tide, in about three hours.

Secure behind their concrete defences, the gunners could afford to wait behind the 100mm howitzers with which they were equipped. They would destroy the ships, one by one as they came into range.it would be like shooting ducks in a shooting gallery.

It was at about this point that the first wave of bombers appeared from unseen carriers over the horizon. Owens thanked his lucky stars for the distraction and, unable to see anybody ashore, climbed up the beach and into the first cover he could find.

Behind him, his track through the mud glared at him but there was nothing he could do about that. The next tide would remove it, he could only hope that it hadn't been spotted by then.

He lay still, watching as one flight of the bombers flew over the island towards the city itself and another peeled off to take out the guns on this island and those on Wolmi-do, the main citadel defending the entrance to the harbour.

Five thirty, nothing had moved on the island. He lifted himself out of his hole and bent almost double to reduce his silhouette, he zig zagged towards the village.

As he approached the village, a group of small children ran out, chasing a run-away kite and surrounded him. The kite retrieved, he was led still crouching in the middle of the group into the village.

"Hallo English. I can't decide whether you're very brave or very stupid. Perhaps when this is all over, we can discuss it over a beer or two?"

"Hallo Lieutenant Yo. It's nice to see you again. Thanks for the welcoming party, I wondered how I was going to get into the village without being seen."

"We've been watching you since early this afternoon. There was a moment, just before the planes came over, that we thought the army had seen you too but if they had, they decided that they were safer in their bunkers than out in the open. Nice timing, did you arrange that?"

"Alas, I'm not that powerful but the good Lord looks after children, idiots and drunks so I reckon I'm in with a chance."

"Ah English, but you only have the one God. We have many."

"Then let us pray that yours are on my side too, eh?"

The Longhouse was warm and dry and clean, dry clothes were found for him. All around, the normal life of the village continued offering the soldiers no indication that their island had been invaded, even by one man.

Food was produced and Lieutenant Yo's wife joined them while they ate.

Darkness fell at about ten and plans were laid. Yo and Owens would take the leading boat and the rest would follow, slowly working their way towards the cleared channel. The fishing lights were well supplied with paraffin and checked to ensure that none failed at a crucial moment.

"I could make a habit of this, you know." Owens lay back in the sampan, a fishing line dangling over the side into the pool of light shed by the vapour lamp.

"Perhaps you should when this is all over. How long do you reckon you can go on playing superman and getting away with it?"

"A few years yet, I hope."

"If I were you, English, I'd make good and sure I got promoted out of harm's way just as soon as I could. This is my country and I don't mind dying for it if necessary but you're twelve thousand miles from home, fighting someone else's battles and in very real danger of paying for it with your life.

"Why would any sane man do that?"

"Ah, Yo, there you have it, or very probably. It's the bit about being sane you see. Were the British sane, there would never have been a British Empire you see. Now, the present socialist government may be giving away or simply losing the empire but it takes generations to breed out the genes that make young men go in search of adventure. And, Yo, I can assure you that there ain't a lot of adventure left in England. The place is overrun with bureaucrats, time servers, petty clerks and nosey bastards and nobody in his right mind would want to be there now."

"So, here you are?"

"So, here I am."

"Well, I'm not ungrateful but I shall be glad when the United Nations gives Korea back to the Koreans. All I want them to do is to restore the Republic and go home. If they like, they can leave a few observers behind to hold the ring whilst we Koreans sort out our own problems but I have no desire to become part of some new, UN empire; that's not what I'm fighting for."

"Be of good heart Sir, I have no intention of colonising Korea. You've had Japanese overlords since the early thirty's, a brief over-lordship by the Americans between forty five and forty nine and by one remove, Russian over-lordship since the invasion. You may take my word for it, I have no desire to prolong your agony."

"I'm sure I can English but you are not in charge of this bean feast and I don't trust that American old man who is in charge. He belongs to the wrong generation, the generation that fought their way from island to island across the pacific simply because the Japanese attacked their base in Pearl Harbour. Had they bombed Tokyo, that would have made sense but they didn't, they used Pearl Harbour as an excuse to conquer every island between Pearl and Japan. Those islands had never been American and they had no business turning them into a military fairground.

"To the islanders, it made very little difference who claimed to be in charge, all they wanted to do was fish, farm and fornicate, though I may have got that in the wrong order."

"You've spent some time thinking about this haven't you?"

"My father was an officer in the Imperial Japanese Army and I had a very good education. I was glad, philosophically, to be rid of the Japanese in nineteen forty five but that didn't mean that everything that they did was wrong. They threw the French out of Indo China and the Brits out of Malaya and Borneo, the Americans out of the Philippines and the Dutch out of Indonesia and replaced them with an Asian hegemony; a Co-Prosperity Zone from which, had the Americans not interfered, the natives as you called them would have benefited. Now, the French are back in Indo China, the Brits in Malaya, the Yanks in the Philippines and the Dutch in Indonesia but it can't last you know, it can't last. The so-called natives now know that the Europeans can be beaten, they will rise up against you and drive you all out again. Mark my words."

207

"You may well be right and what's more, it may be right for these countries to achieve independence but Communism doesn't offer that. Communism offers a nineteenth century solution to what was essentially a European problem. Communism grew out of the Tsarist Russian pogroms against the Jews. All the originators of communism were Jewish and Marx himself was living safely in England at the time. It's bullshit Yo, and dangerous bullshit at that.

"Look at Eastern Europe since the end of the war. Where is their independence, their democracy? It doesn't exist so, you and I will fight together to free the Republic of Korea from the communist invasion and then you can sort out your differences between yourselves. Just don't ask me to come and do it again, eh?"

"Ah, an honest Englishman at last. That sounds like a genuine opinion not the saccharin nonsense we used to get from the British Embassy. I like you English and I respect you; you are an honest man."

"In that case Yo, do you think you could like me and respect me as a Scotsman? We hate the English too."

The darkness was complete. The tide only just on the turn and most of the sampans had moved slowly whilst fishing into their allocated positions. Lieutenant Yo Kim Nee turned out his light and headed seawards to rendezvous with the incoming destroyers.

* * *

Inchon, one hundred and eighty miles behind the front line of the North Korean army investing the Pusan perimeter and even with its defenders reduced by the need to send them south to the invasion at Kunsan, was still not going to be an easy ride for the invading UN troops. To carry out this operation, MacArthur had had to withdraw troops from Pusan, thus endangering what little was left of Korea in allied hands but the 'five Dollar gamble' was worth the risk.

By dawn, British destroyers were in position to the north of Inchon harbour and Americans were in position to the south. From early in the afternoon, large British and American warships anchored to seaward of the islands, poured thousands of high explosive shells into the waiting shore defences. Particular attention was paid to the heavily fortified island of Wolmi-do that formed the pivot between the northern causeway from the mainland and the mole enclosing the second, seaward side of the outer, tidal basin.

During the afternoon, the bombardment continued without pause and six inch shells from the British cruiser HMS Jamaica detonated the defender's main ammunition dump. This caused the biggest explosion of the entire action and, no doubt, substantially reducing the invader's subsequent casualties.

This blanket bombardment was observed to be taking out the fixed gun emplacements, both those previously identified by Lieutenant Owens and those spotted by the constantly over-flying aircraft. The American and British destroyers, lying inside the off-shore islands and dangerously close to the defending army's mobile guns, also maintained a constant bombardment of the shore-line destroying anything that moved or looked even remotely like a defensive position.

Throughout the long day the British and American cruisers, together with the battleship Missouri, The Mighty Mo, maintained, the over-lopping barrage. The heavy fire crept slowly inland, progressively destroying the port's fuel tanks, the town's power station and its road and rail services.

Aircraft from the HMS Triumph acted as gunnery spotters for the big ships whilst the American aircraft attacked anything and everything that they could see.

At dawn on the fifteenth, on the flood tide, US Marines were the first troops to go ashore; overwhelming the North Korean garrison on Wolmi-do. This daring assault allowed subsequent groups to land unmolested and complete the capture of this strategic island but the by then once more receding tide exposed several miles of mud and the main invasion had to wait for the following high tide.

Bombardment of Red Beach, to the north of the causeway and of Blue Beach to the south of the harbour's outer basin continued throughout this second day and American aircraft bombed and strafed the nearby airfield at Kimpo, the main North Korean air force base. In pre-war times, this had been the airport for the Republic of Korea's capital at Seoul.

As the day wore on, individual guns crews aboard the destroyers were stood down for rest and refreshment in readiness for the final close shore bombardment which would precede the landing of the main invasion forces on the beaches either side of the already taken Wolmi-do

As dusk fell and the tide returned, the landing craft formed up and, at the signal from Admiral Doyle, Commander in Chief of the landings, they moved towards the beaches, watched by the destroyers and supported by the most intense bombardment since World War Two.

In Challenger's 'A' gun, Able Seaman Arthur, happy in his work, burst into song in support.

"From the hills of Montezuma to the shores of Tripoli
they're jolly good kids in harbour but oh, my Christ
at sea.
With a bottle of Pepsi-Cola
and a bloody great tub of ice cream,
There's nothing in this world
quite like a United States Marine."

The gunnery officer, Sub. Lieutenant Horton, pressed the transmit button on his microphone.

"A' gun. Tell Able Seaman Arthur to shut up!"

THE NEXT CHALLENGE

CHINA SEA
CHALLENGER

After successfully carrying out secret operations prior to the UN invasion of Korea at Inchon, HMS Challenger is on her way south to Singapore for a long overdue major refit.

This idyll is broken by orders to divert to find, intercept and arrest a clandestine shipment of arms and ammunition en-route to the South China Sea island of Redang for collection by the communist terrorists fighting the British in Malaya.

Unknown to both the British army and to Challenger, the terrorists are preparing to initiate a major push against the British and to establish communist control of a large area of north eastern Malaya; to be recognised and supported by communist governments as an independent Peoples' Republic.